Focus on Sport

ISSUES

Volume 118

Series Editor

Craig Donnellan

Assistant Editor

Lisa Firth

Independence

Educational Publishers
Cambridge

First published by Independence
PO Box 295
Cambridge CB1 3XP
England

© Craig Donnellan 2006

British Library Cataloguing in Publication Data
Focus on Sport – (Issues Series)
I. Donnellan, Craig II. Series
306.4'83

ISBN 1 86168 351 0

Printed in Great Britain
MWL Print Group Ltd

Layout by
Lisa Firth

Cover
The illustration on the front cover is by
Bev Aisbett.

CONTENTS

Chapter One: Sporting Trends

Chapter Two: Sport and Inclusion

Chapter Three: Drug Abuse in Sport

Introduction

Focus on Sport is the one hundred and eighteenth volume in the **Issues** series. The aim of this series is to offer up-to-date information about important issues in our world.

Focus on Sport looks at current sporting trends, diversity and inclusion in sport and the problem of drug use in sport.

The information comes from a wide variety of sources and includes:
Government reports and statistics
Newspaper reports and features
Magazine articles and surveys
Website material
Literature from lobby groups
and charitable organisations.

It is hoped that, as you read about the many aspects of the issues explored in this book, you will critically evaluate the information presented. It is important that you decide whether you are being presented with facts or opinions. Does the writer give a biased or an unbiased report? If an opinion is being expressed, do you agree with the writer?

Focus on Sport offers a useful starting-point for those who need convenient access to information about the many issues involved. However, it is only a starting-point. Following each article is a URL to the relevant organisation's website, which you may wish to visit for further information.

*****

Popularity of lifestyle sports growing fast

Report highlights sports' potential to contribute to getting the nation more active

Sport England this week published research highlighting an increase in the number of lifestyle sports in the past twenty years, as well as a recent surge in participation levels.

The report *Lifestyle Sports and National Sport Policy: An Agenda for Research* summarises available research on lifestyle or so-called 'extreme' sports. It shows that while these sports are particularly popular among 16 to 24-year-olds, they are also growing in popularity among older people. The report cites research showing that the percentage of adults participating regularly increased from 2.5% to 5% between 2001 and 2003. Some 12% of adults want to try lifestyle sports – equivalent to around 5.8 million people.

The percentage of adults participating regularly in lifestyle sports increased from 2.5% to 5% between 2001 and 2003

Sport England provides advice to lifestyle sports on a range of issues such as health and safety, coaching and volunteers – all of which are vital to future growth. The organisation has also supported a number of projects around the country, for example through lottery investments into climbing facilities and skate parks. The report points to ways in which these lifestyle sports may contribute further to the national

SPORT ENGLAND

sports agenda, particularly in terms of the drive to increase participation in sport and physical activity.

Roger Draper, Chief Executive of Sport England, said: 'Sport England is working hard to make England a more active and successful sporting nation. It's clear that lifestyle sports have a huge potential to contribute to this drive and could reap significant rewards for the health of the nation. They are a great way of engaging young people in particular – including many who have dropped out of traditional sport.

'Sport England already supports lifestyle sports in a range of ways and going forward we are keen to

build these links further. We are looking at what other support we can provide, for example by integrating lifestyle sports into multi-sport hubs and, through our advocacy work, encouraging local authorities to think creatively about getting people active and including provision for lifestyle sports in their plans.'

Lifestyle Sports and National Sport Policy: An Agenda for Research also emphasises the important economic contribution made by lifestyle and extreme sports through activity holidays. In 2001 these accounted for between 8% and 15% of the domestic holiday market – worth some £300 million to the economy.
5 April 2005

■ The above information is reprinted with kind permission from Sport England. Visit www.sportengland. org for more information.
© *Sport England*

Youngsters play the game – and avoid trouble

More than 400,000 young people in the United Kingdom will participate in activities at a national network of 3,500 different sporting clubs during the Christmas holidays. Most of the clubs are in less-than-affluent neighbourhoods of our inner-cities, sprawling suburbs and satellite towns.

Clubs for Young People, a voluntary youth organisation, aim to do four things – support, champion, challenge and invest in young people. They offer teenagers real alternatives to carrying out anti-social behaviour and crime, often by giving them a part to play in the community. They try to educate club members about common teenage concerns, such as pregnancy, drug abuse, crime, bullying and health, by using sport as a means of inclusion and inspiration.

93 per cent of schoolchildren involved in the youth organisation regard their club as a safe place in the community, and 84 per cent think going to the clubs keeps them out of trouble

One 15-year-old London schoolboy said that he had been a difficult child before his interest in sport led to him joining one of the clubs. 'I was a nightmare – tormenting old ladies, making kids' lives a misery. No one trusted me except the club leader, who asked me to help him out. I couldn't believe it. He even let me look after the money. Now I'm 15 and the club treasurer, and I help out every day after school.'

By Gareth A Davies

Research carried out by the CYP and Brunel University found that 93 per cent of schoolchildren involved in the youth organisation regard their club as a safe place in the community, and 84 per cent think going to the clubs keeps them out of trouble.

The CYP's Do Somethin' campaign aims to give a further 120,000 teenagers responsible roles in clubs and communities over the next three years. Many of the youngsters will go on to work towards Community Sports Leader Awards.

Last week, the CYP held their senior boxing finals at a gala dinner in London attended by former boxers Alan Minter, Barry McGuigan and Michael Watson.

Among the audience was Anthony Ogogo, 17, one of Britain's brightest boxing talents, who has won gold medals as a middleweight at the Junior Olympics and World Cadet Championships. He hopes to compete at the Beijing Olympics. Ogogo, speaking at the gala, said the CYP regard him as a good role model because his A-level studies – performing arts, PE, biology and media studies – have not suffered because of his dedication to boxing, which involves training three times a day.

Tony Cesay, who is at the other end of the scale from Ogogo, was also in the audience at the gala. Cesay, 39, boxed for England as an amateur for many years, but chose never to turn professional. He now works with schoolchildren in Beckton, east London, where he helps to improve their lives.

He has even set up his own Academy of Sport and Performing Arts, which has received Government funding. 'Using Sport As a Tool for Education is my motto,' Cesay said. And he should know, because he came up the hard way. Originally from Sierra Leone, he has never forgotten his roots. Apart from his work with east London schools, he has continued to help teenagers in Sierra Leone known as 'toy soldiers', who were turned into killers aged just 10 and 11 because of the African country's bloody civil conflict.

Cesay, a former ABA national champion, said: 'My projects are about developing young people for life ahead. The project focuses on sports education and difficulties which can be spotted early. I think that prevention is better than cure. Dealing with a problem before it grows too big means that you have to do less to fix it. The academy uses sport to assist children in building their confidence, and communication skills, which in turn benefits the neighbourhood and community in the long run.'

Great words, great work.

23 December 2005

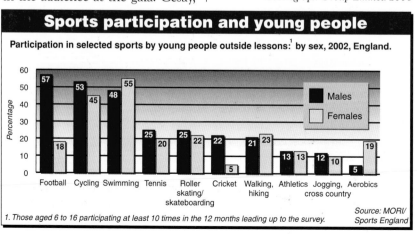

Sports participation and young people

Participation in selected sports by young people outside lessons:[1] by sex, 2002, England.

1. Those aged 6 to 16 participating at least 10 times in the 12 months leading up to the survey.

Source: MORI/ Sports England

School sports

PE, School Sport and Club Links (PESSCL)

What is PE, School Sport and Club Links (PESSCL)?

PE, School Sport and Club Links (PESSCL) is a government strategy launched in April 2003. The aim of PESSCL is to increase the number of children and young people aged between 5 and 16 who take up and enjoy sporting opportunities within and beyond the curriculum. The target is to increase the number of school children in England who spend a minimum of four hours each week on high quality PE and school sport to 85% by 2008.

By building on and improving the quality of existing PE and school sport opportunities available to young people in schools it is hoped that an increasing proportion of children will be guided into local sports national governing body (NGB) affiliated and accredited clubs. The strategy aims to promote a culture that enables and values the full involvement of every child and young person, whether as a competitor, volunteer, official or organiser. It is hoped that this will lead to a significant increase in the number of young people taking part in high quality club sport on a regular basis.

PESSCL is delivered on a local level through collaboration between School Sport Partnerships, County Sports Partnerships and sports clubs accredited as meeting recognised national minimum standards by the NGBs to which they are affiliated.

More information on the national strategy for PE, School Sport and Club Links is available from: www.teachernet.gov.uk/pe

Why is PE important?

All children should be able to enjoy physical activity whatever their circumstances or abilities, and for many this opportunity is only available to them through school. For those children who demonstrate abilities or talents within the PE curriculum and in school sporting activities, strong links into

Child Protection in Sport Unit

community and club sport should support their development through clear pathways into competitive and/or elite sport.

Physical activity has been shown to have wide-ranging benefits for all children and young people during their school years including improved concentration, commitment and raised self-esteem. It is also strongly linked to improvements in pupil behaviour, school attendance and attainment. PE helps children to develop social skills including teamwork and leadership skills.

Children involved in sport often perform better academically

Physical activity has undisputed long-term health benefits including a reduction in obesity and improved general fitness leading to a reduction in the risk of some health problems including coronary heart disease, diabetes and some forms of cancer. These benefits are particularly significant if a child's experience of physical activity is high quality and fun, motivating them to adopt an active lifestyle and to continue to participate in sport outside of school and into adulthood.

The educational curriculum for PE is now broadly based, providing pupils with a grounding in games, gymnastics, athletics and outdoor adventurous activities. Teaching of PE incorporates the use of information technology (IT) and

focuses upon the development of decision-making skills. PE remains compulsory through all four Key Stages of the national curriculum because of the many benefits for pupils and the aim is to make PE attractive to all children, whatever their level of skill.

For indicators of high quality PE provision go to the DfES guidance document, 'Do you have high quality PE and sport in your school?' at http://www.teachernet.gov.uk/teachingandlearning/subjects/pe/publications/

Why is sport important to children?

Sport helps children and young people to grow healthily and develop personally, socially, emotionally and physically. It can provide them with opportunities to have an enormous amount of fun and increase their circle of friends. Also, by being supported in setting and achieving their own goals in sport, young people can overcome the impact of challenges and barriers in other areas of their lives.

Through sport children can develop valuable qualities including leadership, independence, cooperation, confidence and self-esteem. Research has shown that children involved in sport often perform better academically and have greater social confidence.

Sport can enrich people's quality of life, raise self-esteem and confidence levels and provide enjoyment to individuals.

It also has a much larger part to play in building stronger, safer communities, strengthening the economy and developing the skills of local people, meeting the needs of children and improving everyone's health.

■ Information from the Child Protection in Sport Unit. Visit www.thecpsu.org.uk for more.
© NSPCC

Only a quarter of pupils take part in a team sport

**By Sarah Harris,
Education Correspondent**

Most pupils fail to take part in regular competitive sports matches at primary and secondary schools, a study has found.

Only one in four is competing against other teams within their school in sports such as hockey and netball.

The research, commissioned by the Department for Education and Skills, shows that the figures are worst among some of the country's Left-wing councils.

Competitive sport has been squeezed out partly because of the politically correct attitude that 'all must have prizes'.

This is despite repeated promises from Labour to put such activities at the heart of the curriculum.

The poll of almost 11,500 primary and secondary schools taking part in a Government scheme to improve sporting opportunities reveals there is still a long way to go.

And the nationwide picture is likely to be even bleaker because schools involved in the £820million sports programme have the best PE provision.

The study, by research group TNS, found that fewer schools offered team sports such as netball, hockey, rounders and volleyball this year than last.

Overall, in a typical week only 25 per cent of pupils were involved in 'intra-school' competitive activities such as playing against other teams in inter-house championships.

In primary schools, the level of participation was 23 per cent and in secondaries, 28 per cent. Pupils aged nine to 13 were most likely to take part in these competitive activities.

In a typical week only 25 per cent of pupils were involved in 'intra-school' competitive activities such as playing against other teams in inter-house championships

The survey found that in terms of inter-school competition – where pupils take on children from other schools – primaries were more likely to be involved than secondaries.

The Isle of Wight and North Lincolnshire, both Tory councils, had the highest percentage of pupils involved in inter-school competitions, at 57 per cent and 51 per cent respectively.

Labour councils in London were among the worst, including Tower Hamlets, at 25 per cent; Hackney 21 per cent; and Lewisham and Haringey, both 24 per cent.

Nick Seaton, of the Campaign for Real Education, said some councils still had an 'ideological objection' to competitive sport.

'Ministers keep shouting about competitive sport but they're not doing anything serious about it,' he said. 'Parents and employers will be shocked by the low levels participating in schools.

'Youngsters have to learn to compete when they go out into the real world and not doing so leaves them unprepared.'

An education department spokesman denied that only a quarter of pupils did any competitive sport.

He added: 'We are firmly in favour of competitive sport and the reality is that over a third of children are involved in competitions against other schools.'

Last August, Culture Secretary Tessa Jowell declared it was time to overturn the 'politically correct nonsense of the Eighties that competition damages children'.

But critics say the selling-off of playing fields and the growth of non-competitive games have helped create the problem.

■ This article first appeared in the *Daily Mail*, 29 November 2005.

More sports playing fields created than ever before

Information from the Department for Culture, Media and Sport

New figures show that more new sports facilities are being created and, for the first time, the number of playing fields is growing. The Department for Culture, Media and Sport and Sport England released the 2003/04 figures today, which reveal that applications regarding playing fields in England are resulting in more new sports facilities and less non-sports projects.

The statistics show that of the 959 applications that were approved for development, 590 involved projects that would greatly improve the quality of sport on offer at the site. These include new sports centres, tennis courts, athletics tracks and AstroTurf pitches, as well as changing rooms and floodlights. They also include 132 cases where like-for-like replacement playing fields were provided.

Of the 959 approved applications, just 52 (4%) were deemed to be detrimental to sporting provision – 31 of which were owned by local authorities and 21 owned privately. This is against a backdrop of some 44,000 playing pitches across 21,000 sites in England, and the creation in 2003-04 of 72 additional new playing fields. 314 applications were approved for development on sites, which were too small to accommodate playing pitches. In only two cases was there a complete loss of a playing field.

Sports Minister Richard Caborn welcomed the statistics, saying: 'I am pleased with these figures. More playing fields are being created or improved than being lost and this shows that we are starting to turn the tide on the playing field issue. Not only are we losing fewer fields to non-sporting development but we are also creating the facilities that people need to play the sport they want.

'New indoor and outdoor facilities are now cropping up every week – from indoor basketball courts and newly laid grass rugby fields to all-weather floodlit football pitches. We are ensuring that if a development on a playing field is approved, sport has to be the winner.

'But we are not complacent. There is always more to do and the Government is continuing to work to further improve the protection afforded to playing fields.'

Strict regulations are in place that mean Sport England scrutinise every application involving a playing field and, if there is a loss for sport arising from a development, then they will object to the application. And rules agreed between DfES and the NPFA last year ensure that any sale must be an absolute last resort – and that the proceeds must be used to improve outdoor sports facilities wherever possible.

For the first time, the number of playing fields is growing

The new figures were also welcomed by the National Playing Fields Association. Don Early, Deputy Director of the NPFA, said: 'The NPFA welcomes this announcement and the overall net increase in playing fields demonstrated in these statistics. This reflects the positive moves taken by Government. The latest statistics however mix improvements to playing fields with threats and losses and I believe there is work to be done to redress the balance of investment back from indoor to outdoor sports facilities.

'Right now over 65% of £207m of planned investment is directed toward indoor facilities, at a time when pitch improvements and ancillary outdoor facilities are badly needed. Specifically, at a time when we are trying to increase the number of youngsters and women involved in more sport, we need to make sure there's also a focus on adequate changing facilities. Part of the solution is for the Government, through the ODPM and DCMS, to require all local authority-held playing fields to be granted similar protection to that afforded by the DfES to school playing fields.'

The Minister for Sport continued: 'We note the suggestions made by the NPFA and are working with the ODPM and others to continue to build on the positive work we have done already.'

ODPM Minister Baroness Andrews said: 'The Government requires local planning authorities to protect the playing fields and other forms of open space that their communities need. Hence we expect them to take full account of the importance of recreational space in their planning decisions and in their new-style local plans.'

Roger Draper, Chief Executive of Sport England, said: 'Sport England's main objective is to give people more opportunities to get active. A big part of this work is giving people access to the best facilities, whether it be a regenerated playing field or a state-of-the-art AstroTurf. These figures are particularly pleasing as it shows that our joint work to ensure playing fields are protected and enhanced is paying off.'
22 July 2005

■ Information from the Department for Culture, Media and Sport. Visit www.culture.gov.uk for more information.

Lost – 34,000 playing fields

Information from the National Playing Fields Association

Closer examination of new figures released by the Government show that England has lost more playing fields in recent years than anybody realised.

Over the last 13 years, according to figures quoted by Sports Minister Richard Caborn, nearly 34,000 sports pitches across England have disappeared.

'These figures are truly appalling. We have been saying for years that the situation was bad, but it is far worse than anyone suspected,' said Mrs Alison Moore-Gwyn, Director of the National Playing Fields Association.

Mr Caborn quoted the statistics in a press release aimed at showing the situation was starting to improve. He said there were now 44,000 playing pitches in England, 72 of which had been created last year. Earlier Sports Council statistics announced in 1994 but collected two years earlier showed that there were 77,949 sports pitches spread over 25,940 sites in England. By 2005, according to Mr Caborn's latest figures, that tally had shrunk to 44,000 pitches on 21,000 sites.

'Even allowing for the few new fields that have been created in the last 13 years, we have lost nearly 45% of our stock of sports pitches. By any standards, this is a shameful record,' said Mrs Moore-Gwyn.

'We at the NPFA are delighted that there have been some small improvements, and of course we are always pleased when new playing fields and sports pitches are created. But Mr Caborn's own figures show how both Conservative and Labour Governments have allowed a creeping disaster to overtake playing fields throughout England.'

Exact figures have still not been released to show the situation in Scotland, Wales, or Northern Ireland.

NATIONAL PLAYING FIELDS

'This is not a party political point. Since 1992, when the figures were collected, we have had five years of Conservative government, and eight years of Labour,' said Mrs Moore-Gwyn. 'Mr Caborn says he is beginning to turn the tide, and we welcome that. But the tide he is trying to turn has been running far more strongly for the last thirteen years than anyone in government has appreciated. It has devastated our stock of playing fields.'

The Government has estimated previously that 40 sites a month were being lost under the Conservatives – a total of 2,400 sites over their five years in power. That means that according to Mr Caborn's figures, 2,540 sites have gone while Labour has been in control.

'This is the first time that the Government has released figures like this, and it shows how urgently we need to have regular, reliable, and transparent statistics about the loss of playing fields. Mr Caborn will continue to have our support in anything he does to try to reverse this trend – but neither Labour nor the Conservatives have anything in their record to be proud of so far. In 13 years, this country appears to have squandered nearly half of our children's inheritance,' Mrs Moore-Gwyn said.

1 August 2005

■ The above information is reprinted with kind permission from the National Playing Fields Association. Visit www.npfa.co.uk for more information.

© NFPA

Playing field gains

Playing field gains – regional breakdown of new facilities to be provided. Comparison figures 2002/03 and 2003/04.

Region	2002/03		2003/04	
	Number of new facilities	Planned investment	Number of new facilities	Planned investment
East	44	£29,599,000	29	£14,767,000
East Midlands	41	£26,286,000	37	£23,415,000
London	50	£33,218,200	63	£65,213,272
North East	59	£23,374,000	62	£28,732,000
North West	55	£30,440,000	46	£19,511,000
South East	50	£31,250,000	94	£51,761,000
South West	44	£29,759,000	118	£47,582,499
West Midlands	78	£42,703,000	67	£44,077,000
Yorkshire	68	£21,925,000	60	£21,887,500
Total	**489**	**£268,554,000**	**576**	**£316,946,271**

Source: Department for Culture, Media and Sport. Crown copyright.

Whatever happened to football hooliganism?

By Iain Hollingshead

Sports fans often seek to emulate the heroes they come along to watch. Wimbledon spectators are svelte and tanned, rugby supporters are burly and gregarious, crowds at Test match cricket are capable of drinking for almost as long as Andrew Flintoff.

Football, on the other hand, the world's self-styled 'beautiful game', has always attracted a fringe element of fan violence at odds with the increasing metrosexuality of the players themselves. Football hooliganism in this country became widespread in the 70s and 80s with the notorious 'firms' – including the Chelsea Headhunters and the Salford Reds of Manchester United. It reached its peak with the riots that followed the Luton v Millwall encounter in 1985. Ted Croker, then head of the Football Association, was summoned to an audience with Margaret Thatcher. The police even considered suspending domestic football for a season.

A massive police operation was mounted prior to the Euro 1988 championships in Germany to prevent potential hooligans travelling abroad. After the Hillsborough disaster in 1989, stadiums became all-seated, with better stewarding and widespread CCTV, further assisting authorities trying to crack down on hooliganism.

Today, serious incidents at domestic games are largely a matter of the past. Home Office statistics published earlier this month showed that football-related arrests fell by 11% to 3,628 last year, an average of only 1.21 a game. Stringent banning orders continued to be passed in England and Wales, bringing the banning total to 3,153. The Scots held a conference in October looking at the possibility of introducing similar measures.

Abroad, English fans have faced a longer journey towards improving their image. While the excesses of the Scottish 'tartan army' are laughed off as high jinks, the English are still viewed as suitable targets for opposing fans and foreign police forces. The Belgian police were accused by fans of overreacting to the tiniest incidents at Euro 2000. During Euro 2004, there were concerns at one point that England might be thrown out of the competition for something other than penalty misses when 32 fans were arrested in one night on the Algarve. Tony Blair said the rioters 'brought shame on our country'.

Many supporters complain that these incidents are blown out of proportion by the media. The Uefa director of communications actually praised English fans' conduct during Euro 2004 and gave them 'nine out of 10 for behaviour'. There were only six arrests made last year at overseas England matches.

The media have even been accused of inciting the violence. The former *Mirror* editor Piers Morgan had to apologise for his front-page headline, 'Achtung Surrender!' during Euro 96 and his pastiche of Neville Chamberlain's 1939 declaration: '*Mirror* declares football war on Germany'.

More recently, one fan claims, 'I was approached by a photographer from an English tabloid who said he'd give me £150 to kick in a German. I told him where to get off.' Another says he was paid to wrap himself in the flag of St George, lie on the pavement and pretend to be drunk.

'The media love the footage of the perceived scum of society fighting one another,' says the football writer Dougie Brimson. But football-related violence continues to simmer away under the surface, he says. 'The power of the majority needs to be harnessed better to control it,' he says. The real test will come next year, at Euro 2006 in Germany. Police sources say that more than 5,000 banning orders will be in place by then. Reining in the tabloid appetite for a scrap might be harder.

19 November 2005
© Guardian Newspapers Limited 2005

Football-related violence season 2003-04

- Arrests for football-related offences down by 10%, to 3,982 from 4,413
- Level of arrests reflects the lingering domestic football disorder problems
- Substantial increase in the number of football banning orders, up to 2,596 on 18 October 2004, from 1,794 on 14 August 2003
- Targeted police operations resulted in hundreds of high quality football banning orders. 1,263 new bans were made between 15 August 2003 and 18 October 2004
- Arrest levels remain low – the highest league attendances for 34 years, 29,197,510 produced 3,010 arrests – an arrest rate of 0.01%
- Vast majority of matches remain trouble-free – 50% of Premiership, 72% of 1st Division, 82% of 2nd Division and 89% of 3rd Division matches had one arrest or less. Overall, during the 2003-2004 season there was an average of 1.62 arrests per game
- 57% of the total arrests were made outside of grounds, 85% of arrests for violent disorder outside of grounds
- 25% of matches completely police free
- Arrests of England fans decreased from 261 to 70 reflecting a highly successful Euro 2004 tournament

Football offences – statistical highlights (extract). Crown copyright

'Low-impact' policing key to overcoming hooliganism

Liverpool psychology helps bring peace to European football

'Low impact' policing is the key to overcoming 'hooliganism' at major international football tournaments, according to ESRC-funded research.

It found that while preventing known troublemakers from travelling is important, the way to foster incident-free events is a 'low profile', friendly-but-firm police presence, and dealing with fans on the basis of their behaviour not their reputation.

The study, led by Dr Clifford Stott and Dr Otto Adang of the University of Liverpool School of Psychology, analysed the impact of police tactics on levels of hooliganism at Euro 2004 – the Union of European Football Associations (UEFA) championships held in Portugal in June and July of last year.

Researchers included a team of observers from the Portuguese Police Academy and the Universities of Coimbra, Oporto and Lisbon.

Their report shows that when England supporters are treated from the outset as fans rather than 'hooligans', they see themselves as on the same side as the police, sharing the same interest in preventing violence.

Faced with this 'low profile' policing approach, ordinary fans are more likely to oppose trouble among other supporters through 'self-policing', and to regard themselves as friends with fans from other nations.

The findings give a definite 'thumbs up' to the 'low profile' tactics adopted by Portugal's Public Security Police (PSP), in line with advice given to the force by the Liverpool psychologists before the tournament.

If police were visible and the risk of trouble was thought to be normal, the proportion of uniformed officers visible in the crowd was on average only four per every 100 fans.

Where police were present, they were in standard uniforms rather than full riot gear, and were used simply to monitor fan behaviour. Riot police were positioned close by but deliberately out of sight. They could, however, be quickly on hand if needed.

Extensive use was also made of plainclothes police, deployed wherever fans gathered in large numbers.

When treated as fans rather than 'hooligans', supporters see themselves as on the same side as the police

---

Dr Stott said: 'Importantly, during Euro 2004 there were almost no incidents of disorder recorded during our observations in areas controlled by the PSP.

'In spite of a low visible police presence, incidents with the potential to escalate were responded to quickly and appropriately, and clear limits of behaviour were established which ensured that situations quickly calmed.

'In most of the rare cases where something did occur, interventions were rapid but with very low impact, and most fans didn't even notice that an arrest had been made.'

Preventing known troublemakers from travelling to Portugal was another important factor, says the report, along with initiatives developed by visiting police forces, fan organisations and British Embassy staff.

Even so, it was clear that individuals known as 'hooligans' or acting as such were present.

The Liverpool theories on avoiding trouble are strengthened by the two major incidents which did occur in Albufeira – a town controlled by Portugal's national gendarmerie (GNR), which did not adopt the same tactics as the PSP.

Consequently, concludes the report, the GNR were unable to set limits of behaviour early on, or to differentiate between troublemakers and bystanders when forced to intervene. More fans were drawn in, and trouble escalated.

Dr Stott said: 'Our approach was valid and useful in the planning of a successful tournament. We have also begun to understand that use of overwhelming force may manage conflict in the short term, but over time could entrench "hooligans" within fan culture, and undermine critically important "self-policing" efforts of legitimate fans.'
13 October 2005

■ Information from the Economic and Social Research Council. Please visit www.esrcsocietytoday.ac.uk
© ESRC

Commercialisation in sport

YouGov poll: Sports fans concerned at power of the money men

By Andrew Baker

British sport has been taken out of the hands of the fans who support it, and commercialisation is rampant, according to a survey of the nation's attitudes to sport conducted for the *Daily Telegraph* by YouGov.

An overwhelming majority of sports fans feel that the role money plays has increased in recent years, and most of them regret the development. More than 85 per cent of sports followers believe that wealthy business people, promoters and celebrities have an increasing influence at the expense of the traditional fan.

YouGov asked a sample of subjects representing the demographic characteristics of the United Kingdom whether they considered themselves to be interested in sport. More than 60 per cent of men and 40 per cent of women said that they were either 'very' or 'fairly' interested in sport, and this constituency formed the basis for the detailed survey.

> ### More than 85 per cent of sports followers believe that wealthy business people, promoters and celebrities have an increasing influence at the expense of the traditional fan

Few will be shocked to find that football is the nation's favourite sport, but athletics makes a surprising appearance as the country's second most popular sport, no doubt boosted by the performances of Kelly Holmes and the men's sprint relay team in Athens. Among active participants, swimming, football and tennis lead the way.

The high levels of participation recorded for Olympic sports will help London's attempts to win the Olympic Games of 2012. Bid officials will be able to back up the impressive showing of British fans in Athens with evidence that the nation not only watch sport with enthusiasm but play hard as well.

The survey also reveals the growing influence of the internet as an access point for sports fans. More than half have gone online for sporting information at least 10 times in the past year, and fewer than one fifth of sports followers are internet 'virgins'.

Despite the growing commercial power of individual clubs, support for national teams remains strong, with more than half of sports fans significantly concerned about the plight of their nation's representatives. Scottish fans will be delighted to note that they were found to be slightly more patriotic than their English counterparts.

Racism is regarded as a problem in British sport by three-quarters of fans, but the majority regard it as a minor issue, and more believe that instances of racism are declining than those who see the problem increasing.

But by far the most striking finding of the survey is the huge proportion of fans who believe that their sports are increasingly falling under the control of commercial organisations, be they wealthy oligarchs, television companies or corporate sponsors.

While a huge majority recognise the increasing commercialisation of sport, significantly fewer object to the phenomenon. This may mean that fans do not take issue with the increasing importance of money as long as their sport or their team are getting their share of the funds.

Sports followers will certainly not be expecting the Government to do much about commercialisation, or any other sporting matter. The majority of Britons believe the Government have made very little difference to the sporting life of the nation, and of those who do think they have made a difference, the majority believe it has been negative.

So who is responsible? Hardly anyone knows. Fewer than one in four of the nation's sports fans could correctly identify the Sports Minister.

But perhaps the most reassuring aspect of the survey is the diversity of the fans across all age groups and across all sports. There is little evidence that we lose enthusiasm for sport as we grow older, and participation levels – particularly for tennis and swimming – are maintained well beyond middle age.

21 January 2005

World Cup 2018

Sport – YouGov poll results

YouGov questioned 1616 adults aged 18+ throughout Britain online between 7th and 10th January 2005. The sample was drawn from those respondents who had previously said they were 'Very' or 'Fairly' interested in sports – in either one sport or more than one. The data were then weighted to a previously established 'sports fans' profile.

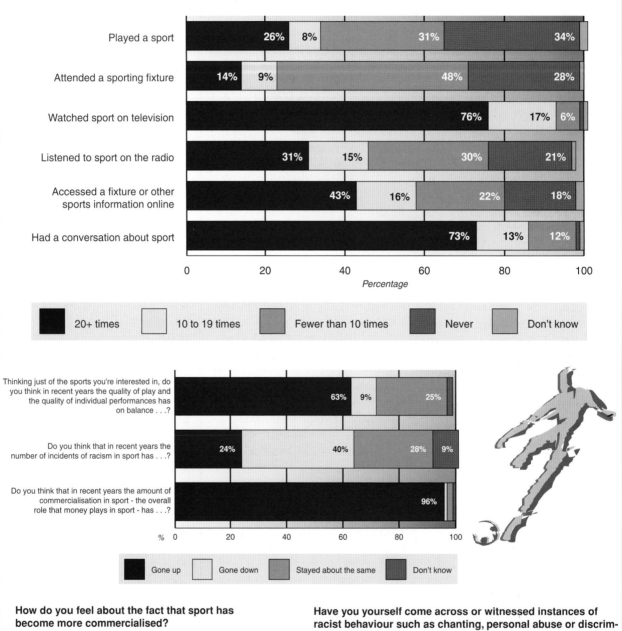

How often in the past year or so have you . . .

	20+ times	10 to 19 times	Fewer than 10 times	Never	Don't know
Played a sport	26%	8%	31%	34%	
Attended a sporting fixture	14%	9%	48%	28%	
Watched sport on television	76%	17%	6%		
Listened to sport on the radio	31%	15%	30%	21%	
Accessed a fixture or other sports information online	43%	16%	22%	18%	
Had a conversation about sport	73%	13%	12%		

Percentage

Legend: 20+ times / 10 to 19 times / Fewer than 10 times / Never / Don't know

	Gone up	Gone down	Stayed about the same	Don't know
Thinking just of the sports you're interested in, do you think in recent years the quality of play and the quality of individual performances has on balance . . .?	63%	9%	25%	
Do you think that in recent years the number of incidents of racism in sport has . . .?	24%	40%	28%	9%
Do you think that in recent years the amount of commercialisation in sport - the overall role that money plays in sport - has . . .?	96%			

Legend: Gone up / Gone down / Stayed about the same / Don't know

How do you feel about the fact that sport has become more commercialised?

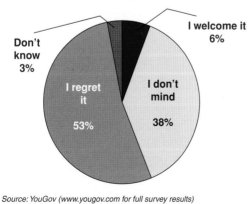

- I welcome it 6%
- Don't know 3%
- I regret it 53%
- I don't mind 38%

Have you yourself come across or witnessed instances of racist behaviour such as chanting, personal abuse or discrimination in the selection of players or club membership?

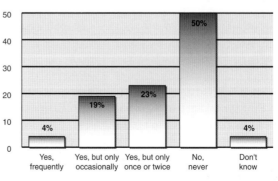

- Yes, frequently 4%
- Yes, but only occasionally 19%
- Yes, but only once or twice 23%
- No, never 50%
- Don't know 4%

Source: YouGov (www.yougov.com for full survey results)

Footballers' pay

Premiership footballers' pay – how much is too much? Information from smile.co.uk

The new football season kicks off in just a couple of weeks' time. But has cash taken over the nation's top sport?

Last year £786 million in wages alone was paid to 2,347 professional footballers, that's roughly equivalent to the GDP of Mongolia in 2005. Of that sum, £583 million went to Premiership players. And the likes of Steven Gerrard and David Beckham are reported to earn over £100,000 A WEEK – that's more than £5 million a year – not bad for playing a bit of footy. But are they worth it?

Are Premiership players paid too much? Should their extortionate wages be given the red card?

Perhaps you think football is easy. After all, how hard can kicking a ball around a pitch be? But then again, these guys are under a lot of pressure to perform. Maybe the pressure they're under justifies their enormous fees. They must perform well both on and off the pitch.

Should these highly paid players have to give a certain percentage of their wages to charity?

Or would you rather see performance-related pay come into effect? If the team does well, or if a particular player does well, should they get a bonus on top of a more conservative salary?

Comments

'£10,000 per week should be a top limit. It's ruining football, violence on the pitch, not enough TV money going to support lesser leagues'
(Mike Collinson)

'It's a business. Fan clubs could attempt to save their members from debt by threatening boycotts for better prices. Rich clubs could be more corporately responsible and support charities.'
(Ian Baker)

'Greedy footballers and stupid chairmen are an obscenity within our national game. Footballers used to get a bit more than the working man, but now they earn more than film stars. Let's have a reality check because ultimately it is the workers of this country who pay

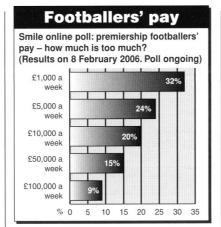

Footballers' pay

Smile online poll: premiership footballers' pay – how much is too much?
(Results on 8 February 2006. Poll ongoing)

Pay	%
£1,000 a week	32%
£5,000 a week	24%
£10,000 a week	20%
£50,000 a week	15%
£100,000 a week	9%

these wages in extortionate admission prices.'
(Terence McGovern)

'No footballer is worth the exorbitant salary they are paid. A short playing career is not an excuse. Even top flight footballers will earn in 5 years, more than I'll earn in a lifetime. The modern world is topsy turvy, but it won't change. Everyone judges and is judged by how much money they earn. We are all guilty in allowing it to happen.'
(Ash)

'£1,000.00 a week is still too much for any sports professional. I think that a large proportion of the profit made through sport should be invested in new sports facilities, working with children and young people to get them involved in sport and a healthy lifestyle, sport support and scholarships for young people from poorer nations and food programmes for poorer nations. All of the richer nations should agree that they will not pay sports professionals high wages and have an agreed international pay scale.'
(Karen)

'The real fans are slowly being edged out of the game through excessive gate and replica kit charges. Sky TV is saturating the viewers with mostly poor performances which will lead to a loss of interest in watching televised matches. International competition is falling behind European club competition and the FA Cup has been devalued. The beautiful game is on a slippery slope oiled by greed.'
(Kevin Murphy)

'Football is a game and is not important. Add me to the £1,000 per week votes. Sewage workers and rat catchers are much more useful and should have some of the excess given to celebrities.'
(Beryl Leslie)

'Millions want to go to watch them, millions want to stay in to watch them, companies want to be associated with them, there is HUGE demand for these people, so economics dictates that they will attract money. So who else should it go to?? Give me a break, these people are the most talented at the biggest sport in the world and they should be rewarded appropriately. The quality of football is one of the things I love about this country, and if we don't pay them, the Italians, Spanish, Japanese, etc. would, and I'd prefer to see the likes of Henry, Ronaldo, Robben, here than elsewhere.'
(Brendan)

'Football players' wages are obscene! They may need a bit extra to secure a living when they no longer play football but the amounts some players earn simply reflect the greedy, corrupt, selfish and cynical nature of the game.'
(Miriam)

'Footballers earn far too much and the game has started to lose its roots. Gone are the days when a working man can afford to take his children to watch the match. The expensive tickets are inflated by the cost of the players' wages. £1000 per week is enough.'
(Peter Thompson)

'Players' wages are definitely too high. How can they justify earning more than most football fans earn in a year in one week? All it does is drive up the cost of supporting your club. Steven Gerrard's wage demands came in the week of G8 with all the talk of Global Poverty – particularly poor timing. Perhaps players should donate 1 week's wages per month to their favourite charity...'
(Rachel)

■ Information reprinted with kind permission from Smile, the Internet bank. Visit www.smile.co.uk for more.
© Smile

Celebrating diversity and inclusion

An extract from the booklet *Ethics in Sport* by Sport Scotland

Everyone has a unique range of skills and knowledge that they bring to sport. An effective organisation recognises this and values its diversity. It acknowledges the benefits of different cultures, abilities and lifestyles in helping to develop the sport and achieve organisational objectives. In terms of recruitment of employees and volunteers, an effective organisation recruits, selects, develops and promotes people according to the needs of the organisation and the capacity to undertake the work required. In terms of participation, it promotes and welcomes the range of talent and knowledge of all individuals involved in the sport and in the wider community.

> *Equity in sport is the practice of fairness and the upholding of social justice to ensure that all individuals are respected, have equal opportunities and have their rights protected*

Acknowledgement and respect for one another are critical to the development and success of sport in Scotland, the UK and across the world. Organisations need to avoid anecdotal comment or statements of assumption and take active steps forward to ask relevant questions and obtain significant data on whether diversity is celebrated and valued within their sporting community.

Equity

Equity is fundamental to the participation in and the governance, organisation and delivery of sport. Equity in sport is the practice of fairness and the upholding of social justice to ensure that all individuals are respected, have equal opportunities and have their rights protected.

Equity is critical to the celebration of diversity in sport. It is no longer acceptable for individuals to negatively discriminate or put down others on the basis of a difference in religion or faith, race or ethnicity, culture, socio-economic status, gender, sexuality, age, disability or any other social or physical categorisation. Nor is it acceptable for individuals to ignore or in any way endorse the behaviour of others who discriminate in such a way.

It is important for all those involved in sport to support and promote the principles of equity, whether they are playing, refereeing, administrating, managing, governing, supporting athletes, sponsoring, spectating, reporting or engaged in any other way in sporting activities.

It is imperative that when incidents of negative discrimination occur they are dealt with swiftly and effectively. It is therefore important that sport organisations each have a clear and comprehensive disciplinary process. A process that is embedded within their constitution and linked directly to all policies, procedures and codes of the organisation, in particular their equity policy.

Sport Scotland fully supports the practice of equity within sport through a range of programmes and resources.

■ The above information is reprinted with kind permission from Sport Scotland. Visit www.sportscotland.org.uk for more information.

© Sport Scotland

Goal: racial equality in football

Summary of research findings – information reprinted with permission from the Commission for Racial Equality

This article summarises the findings of the Commission for Racial Equality's (CRE's) research report, *Racial Equality in Football*, and the resulting action plan.

The research, carried out by Leeds Metropolitan University in 2004, represents a determined effort by the CRE to assess equal opportunities in the football industry. The report is based on an analysis of the responses to a questionnaire sent to 92 FA Premier League and Football League clubs, 43 county football associations, and national bodies such as the Football Association, the Premier League, the Football League, the Football Foundation and the Professional Footballers' Association.

The results show that the football industry, with some exceptions, has not taken the question of equality of opportunity seriously. The CRE is committed to working with the industry to put this right.

Key findings

- Ethnic minorities are severely under-represented in the boardrooms and governance arrangements of football clubs and national football organisations. Only one FA Premier League club reported having a non-white board director. There are no non-white members of the FA board or the 92-strong FA council. The under-representation of ethnic minorities extends to the terraces as well.
- Black players predominate at every level of the game, but there are hardly any Asian or Chinese players, at any level or in any age group. For example, in the academies run by the FA Premier League clubs, while there are six times the numbers of black players

COMMISSION FOR RACIAL EQUALITY

compared to their number in the population of England and Wales, Asian and Chinese players are significantly under-represented.

- The vast majority of professional football league clubs do not give their staff any training in equal opportunities.
- In the FA Premier League, only 32% of clubs train their staff; in Division One, 32%; in Division Two, 13%; and in Division Three, 9%.
- Too many clubs, particularly in the lower divisions, still have no equal opportunities policy, and where policies do exist, they tend to be very basic.
- Very few clubs formally monitor the take-up of promotion and training opportunities.
- No national football organisation follows best practice in recruitment and selection.

National football organisations have accepted that they need to change. Last year an All-Agency Review Team was set up to look at questions of ethics and sports equity, with representatives from the Football Association, the Premier League, the Football League, the Professional Footballers' Association, the League Managers' Association and the Football Foundation. The team has agreed a ten-point plan to tackle racism and promote and achieve equality of opportunity in all parts of the industry.

Good, but not enough. The football industry needs to rise to the challenge. It needs targets, and help in order to change.

The CRE has charged two special advisors with this role: Paul Elliott and Garth Crooks, both well qualified by their experience of the football industry to help secure a real commitment to change across the football sector. They will be monitoring and evaluating the response to the targets the CRE has set for the Football Association, the Premier League, the Football League, all clubs in the FA Premier League and Divisions One, Two and Three, as well as the Football Foundation, the Professional Footballers' Association and the county football associations.

- The above information is reprinted with kind permission from the Commission for Racial Equality. Visit www.cre.gov.uk for more information.

© Commission for Racial Equality

Racism alive and kicking in England, say Uefa

In a truly extraordinary outburst, high-ranking official claims problem has been 'swept under carpet'

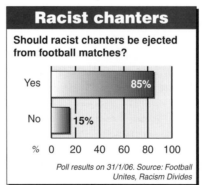

By Anna Kessel

One of UEFA's most senior officials has dismissed British football's success in tackling racism and claimed that racist abuse has declined only because working-class fans have been priced out of attending matches. William Gaillard, Uefa's director of communications, also told *Observer Sport* that there is as much racism in English football as in the Spanish game, where black players such as Barcelona's Samuel Eto'o are regularly targeted, several Primera Liga clubs have been punished for their fans' behaviour and national team manager Luis Aragones has been fined for calling Thierry Henry a 'black shit'. Gaillard also insisted that the racist taunting of England players, primarily Shaun Wright-Phillips and Ashley Cole, during the team's friendly against Spain in Madrid in November 2004 was down to Anglo-Spanish rivalry dating back to the Spanish Armada, rather than outright prejudice. The Uefa official's extraordinary comments drew condemnation from anti-racist campaigners in Britain, who expressed shock at his 'misguided' and 'misjudged' dismissal of 20 years of action, which has won praise worldwide – including from Uefa and Fifa.

Gaillard said: 'In the UK I sometimes get the feeling the issue has been swept under the carpet by raising prices. If you fill the stadiums with middle-class people you have far less problems.'

Comparing football in Spain and England, he added: 'I have been many times in Spain. I would not say that Spain is more racist than England.'

The racist insults that black England players endured at the Bernabeu happened because 'there is a history of hostility between these countries, going back to the Armada, so there are a lot of emotions that have little to do with race. I would not take that incident and say it's more difficult to be black in Spain than it is in England. That would be going too far.'

Gaillard's remarks are surprising because of Uefa's high profile anti-racist stance and because of his work with organisations such as Kick It Out, British football's pioneering anti-racist group. They came when *Observer* Sport asked him to clarify Uefa's view of controversial comments made by the head of the Spanish Football Federation at the end of Uefa's conference on racism last week. Angel Maria Villar Llona, a vice-president of Uefa and Fifa, stunned delegates by declaring that too much attention was being given to racism. 'Let's not make a mountain out of a molehill,' he said.

Then, in a reference to Aragones's insult to Henry, Llona suggested that racist remarks made by players or managers during games should be kept secret. 'Things that take place on the pitch should be left there,' he said. Anti-racism campaigners were shocked by his intervention. Gaillard, who helped Llona prepare his speech, was reluctant to condemn his Uefa colleague's remarks, though he did confirm that Uefa were frustrated at players who complained of racism to the media and then failed to follow up the complaint through the formal procedure. 'It's something we've complained about at Uefa because we want a written statement to take to court and players very often refuse.'

Garth Crooks, the former Tottenham striker who is now a BBC football reporter, said that Gaillard's 'misguided' remarks ignored the reality that many seats at many Premiership clubs, such as Manchester United, are still affordable. 'There is [also] no doubt that in England the fight against racism in football is significantly better than anywhere in Europe,' said Crooks.

Measures to banish the racist abuse that used to disfigure British football – such as CCTV cameras, anti-racist advertising in grounds, messages in match programmes and stewards – showed 'there can be no doubt that we've put a tremendous amount of money, effort and resources into educating the public on anti-racism. William's facts are somewhat off line here.'

Kick It Out director Piara Powar said that Gaillard was wrong to claim that England was no better than Spain at combating racism and said he was defending Llona because he is a senior figure in football politics.

'We do have very high ticket prices. That puts forward this idea that the middle classes aren't racist, but that's just a stereotype that football administrators in particular tap into,' said Powar. 'So I wouldn't accept that. You're as likely to hear racism in hospitality boxes as you are on the terraces.'

5 February 2005

Asians can play football

Another wasted decade

Back to the future: *Asians Can't Play Football* 1996

It is almost a decade since the publication of the ironically named study *Asians Can't Play Football* (1996). Much publicised in the media, this report was then seen as an important breakthrough in articulating both the frustrations and the aspirations of a section of the British community that seemed to be largely alienated by a sport that means so much to them.

The report set out a development plan containing specific recommendations aimed at the professional and amateur game in England, in schools and in the wider community. It argued for much-needed structural changes to address institutional barriers and it called for a pro-active approach in order to accelerate opportunities for Asians as both players and coaches in professional football.

Dialogue was sought with the Football Association hierarchy in 1996 in order to cost the proposals and to agree a list of priorities. Sadly, despite the warm welcome, to date the FA has made too few meaningful attempts to address, directly, the recommendations in the report or to produce a viable alternative strategy of a sort necessary for promoting real opportunities in the game for members of British Asian communities.

The initial response of the Football Association was to host an exploratory national football conference on Asians in football in Oldham (in October 1996) and, subsequently, to convene an Asians in Football working group, with members drawn from Asian communities around Britain. At the time, concerns were expressed among members of this new group about its real purpose and approach and, in particular, if and how its activities would ever feed directly into the governing structures within the Football Association.

Despite its good intentions, formally the group appeared to have had little status within the FA and, therefore, little influence on decision-making processes. Unfortunately, too, the wider impact of the working group has been very limited given the resources made available to it and, more recently, its work has been subsumed within the Football Association's newly established diversity framework.

A changing game?

We accept, of course, that since 1996 the English game has changed dramatically. How could we say otherwise? We have seen the emergence of important new youth structures such as the introduction of Academies at clubs; the publication of Labour's Charter for Football and the government's Task Force; the FA's new Equity strategy; Race Equality Training and Race Equality Standards at Premier League clubs; community projects aimed at increasing Asian involvement; and the appointment of Directors of Football and other new specialist posts at a number of professional clubs.

New football development centres – some in inner-city areas – have also had an impact on young player recruitment. The huge impact on the English game of globalisation and the recruitment of young foreign players has also influenced club recruitment policies and practices. We can even see a smattering of British Asian faces in many major English football stadia today – though it remains a smattering, even in towns and cities where British Asian communities show a very substantial presence.

It might be argued, especially given all the above, that some of the recommendations in *Asians Can't Play Football* have, to an extent at least, been overtaken by events. However, its core conclusions regarding the massive under-representation, lack of access and denial of opportunity for young Asian players, coaches and administrators in football in England, arguably, remains the same. What do we mean by this?

Firstly, change in the active fan base in England has been painfully slow and so, we must conclude, it seems to be a low priority – if a priority at all – for some in the English professional leagues. There are more Asian club fans and more Asian followers of the national team than in 1996, but we still need action in this area to increase numbers.

Secondly, very few people from ethnic minority communities – Asians, British blacks or other visible minorities – work in senior positions inside English clubs and the top leagues, which still seem to be a 'closed shop' at this level to people of colour. And this is despite the game's very public 'embracing' these days of Equal Opportunities Policies.

Thirdly, what is also beyond dispute is the extremely poor representation of potential Asian professional footballers at English clubs, as reflected in a 2004 Commission for Racial Equality (CRE) report on football in England. The CRE noted the hugely disappointing low numbers of young Asians currently attached to club Centres of Excellence or Youth Academies. Back in 1996 we estimated the figure of young Asian players connected to English professional clubs to be a tiny 0.2%, but by late 2004 it had barely improved, rising only to 0.8% in Academies at Premier League Clubs.

No doubt the football authorities will respond to this report – as they do to any such intervention of this kind – by insisting that we have omitted mention of important new initiatives.

Our response, frankly, is: so what? It may feel like the game is changing, and initiatives in the sport may be multiplying, but all the evidence confirms that change in behaviour at the highest levels of the game still lags lamentably behind any real change in attitude or in stated policy. We have had nine years of 'change' in the game since *Asians Can't Play Football*: but are things really that different?

Despite small pockets of good practice, often in difficult circumstances, in various parts of the country – e.g. in London, Leeds, Luton, Bradford and Leicester, etc. – our national sport, acknowledged to be hungrily 'consumed' in all its forms by the British Asian population, is still barely connecting at all with young British Asians interested in pursuing a career in professional football on either the playing or non-playing sides of the fence.

We believe, unequivocally, that this absence remains rooted in systemic failings and, in particular, in the structured inability of too many officials, scouts, coaches and managers to look beyond the negative stereotypical images still held of British Asians, and the aversion of such staff to investigating alternative recruitment methods.

We might also add that it is no defence against charges of racism and exclusion for the game to point to the recruitment of more overseas players of colour if it is wilfully remaining disconnected from minorities at home.

A new agenda

At the local levels of the sport it is sad to report that a few all-Asian local football leagues still exist in England, partly because of a lack of confidence in local FA decision-makers to afford adequate protection against racism and partly because it remains a way in which the community seeks to fill the gap.

They exist, therefore, for a purpose – but we accept they are not the answer to the problem of Asian under-representation in the professional game.

The proliferation of clumsy promotional events and of occasional claims that we have unearthed the next Asian 'superstar', a role model for others to follow, is merely a distraction from the much more pressing need for structural change.

Our agenda, prompted by another decade of wasted opportunities, is to develop a strategic action plan that has a real chance of making some genuine progress. We seem to be decades away from a time when a Zesh Rehman or a Michael Chopra are more than 'novelty value' in the sport, or token Asian players who are wheeled out to demonstrate 'progress'. Instead, they should now be part of a production line, one which is churning out dozens of British Asian football wannabes every year.

All this means that after witnessing too many years of doing it 'your way' we now want to have a go at doing it 'our way'. In recent months we have been developing an action plan for British Asians in English football, one which is both radical and exciting, but it is also one which is largely complementary to the work of the Football Association. We think, after waiting forlornly for so long for change 'from the inside', that its time has now come.

Looking forward – not back

Ten years ago we sought a meaningful partnership with the FA and with the game at large. Our work was publicly warmly welcomed but, ultimately, our requests fell on deaf ears.

Whilst we remain frustrated, we prefer to look forward rather than back because of what is at stake. We owe it to new generations of young British Asian footballers and administrators in this country. The British game will remain the poorer

without their vital contribution at the very top. Both the 'social inclusion' and business case arguments grow stronger as we, in the UK, undergo major demographic changes and, in particular, as many of the heavily urbanised sections of our towns and cities gravitate towards British minority ethnic majority status.

The English game – especially perhaps its technical staff and leaders – has too often shown itself to be reluctant, to engage effectively with 'outside' influences. Removing this barrier, once and for all, will be key to future success for all our sakes.

The future

There is so much still to do in advancing the claims of British Asians in the game. In making our case we also recognise other exclusions. The overall problem of a lack of representation in football is an issue that needs to be addressed at all levels of the sport.

Asians are being denied opportunities as players but former black players – who collectively have given so much to the game – are grossly under-represented as coaches and managers. A different problem but another area in which the game seems to be looking the other way when talented individuals come knocking.

Many community clubs, organisations and volunteers have taken the lead in their local areas, despite the barriers and frustrations they have faced. It is now time for a real Asian revolution in the British game, one which is led and powered from the very top of the professional game.

We must not be so dazzled by the impact of globalisation as to miss the really big story closer to home. British Asians are crying out for change. This time we must make things happen.

Jas Bains

■ The above information is an extract from the introduction to the report *Asians Can Play Football: Another Wasted Decade*, published by the National Asians in Football Forum, September 2005, and reprinted with permission.

© *National Asians in Football Forum*

Football to boot out homophobic fans

After giving racism the red card, the FA is set to target anti-gay taunts

Football fans who hurl anti-gay taunts at players, referees and other supporters will be identified and prosecuted in a new clampdown on behaviour at matches.

Following the success of the drive against racism in the game, the Football Association is making the eradication of homophobia its next priority. Footballers are regularly derided from the stands as 'poofs' or 'queers', for example when they go down injured.

'There is a problem with homophobic abuse in the game directed at not just players but also referees and also opposing fans,' said Lucy Faulkner, the FA's Ethics and Sports Equity Manager. 'Such behaviour is offensive and runs totally counter to both the game's family image and efforts to make football more acceptable to all sectors of society.'

In a bid to banish such behaviour, the FA has expanded the role of its freephone hotline for reporting racist incidents at matches to include homophobic comments. It is also overhauling the training it gives match officials so that referees and their assistants recognise and

By Denis Campbell, Sports News Correspondent

punish such incidents in both the professional and amateur game. Players who use such language may now be shown a red card.

'Homophobic abuse is a breach of Law 12, which covers offensive, insulting and abusive language on the pitch, and is a red card offence,' said Faulkner.

'One referee in grassroots football recently told me that he regularly receives homophobic abuse himself,' she added.

In the most infamous example of homophobia, Liverpool's Robbie Fowler bent over and waved his bottom at Chelsea's Graeme Le Saux. Fowler had already called his opponent a 'poof' earlier in the match in February 1999, to which Le Saux replied: 'But I'm married.' The Liverpool player then said: 'So was Elton John, mate.'

Ex-Norwich City, Nottingham Forest and Hearts striker Justin Fashanu, Britain's only openly gay

player to date, received horrendous abuse during matches in his career in the Eighties and Nineties and later committed suicide.

The FA is holding its first 'homophobia summit' this week. Participants from across the game will be told about the recent conviction – the first of its kind – of a Hull City supporter for hurling anti-gay taunts at Brighton and Hove Albion fans. Hull magistrates' court heard how Kevin Smith had chanted 'indecent' comments at the visiting spectators when Brighton played Hull in August. He was fined £50, ordered to pay £50 costs and banned from attending any Hull City game for three years.

Footballers are regularly derided from the stands as 'poofs' or 'queers', for example when they go down injured

---

Brighton fans are regularly subjected to homophobic abuse simply because the city has a large gay population. 'The other team's fans often chant "Does your boyfriend know you're here?",' said Faulkner. 'That, though, is very much at the milder end of the spectrum.'

Michael Collins, spokesman for the Gay Football Supporters' Network, said: 'Calling someone a "poof" or a "queer" seems to be the last acceptable thing you can shout at people at matches. Most people wouldn't racially abuse a black player any more, but some think that anti-gay taunts are OK.'

30 October 2005

The place of gender equity in sport

The concept and practice of equity is fundamental in women's sport, and needs to underpin all thinking in the sports sector

What is gender equity?

- Equity and equality are often confused. The Equal Opportunities Commission defines equality as: 'having a society where everyone is free from assumptions and discrimination based on factors such as gender, race or disability'.

Equity is not just about treating everyone the same – it may also use positive action initiatives and measures to address existing inequities

---

- Equity is synonymous with fairness and justice. To be equitable means to be fair, and to be seen to be fair. Equity addresses many forms of discrimination on the basis of race, gender, ability, age, national or ethnic origin, religion and sexual orientation. Equity is not just about treating everyone the same – it may also use positive action initiatives and measures to address existing inequities.
- Gender equity is the principle and practice of fair and equitable allocation of resources and opportunities for females and males.
- A primary goal of gender equity is to provide all individuals with access and opportunity to take part in a full range of activities: this enables them to benefit from, excel at and fulfil their human potential.

What does a gender equitable organisation look like?

An organisation which is gender equitable has systems and structures that do not discriminate against women or men. This includes:

- creating opportunities for both women and men to assume leadership roles
- making sure that committees and decision-making working groups have a balance of women and men
- using language and images in publications and promotions that represent women and men positively
- keeping track of gender patterns and trends
- understanding specific issues facing girls and women in sport and using this information to make decisions
- making the workplace and the sporting environment accessible and attractive to women and girls as well as men and boys.

Why is it an issue in sport?

Women are under-represented at all levels of sport:

- in participation rates
- in positions of leadership
- in public recognition
- in employment.

    This is not because of a lack of interest by women, but reflects a long history of direct and indirect forms of discrimination. It is important for men and women to work together to enhance sport for everyone.

What are the benefits of gender equity to a sports organisation?

Sports organisations have much to gain by committing themselves to gender equity in sport. For example:

- it ensures fuller representation of the population base that sport serves
- it increases the talent pool of skilled administrators, coaches and officials

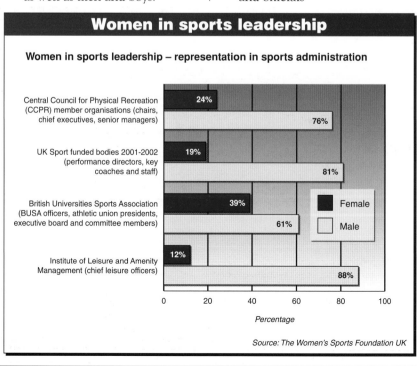

Women in sports leadership

Women in sports leadership – representation in sports administration

Central Council for Physical Recreation (CCPR) member organisations (chairs, chief executives, senior managers): 24% / 76%

UK Sport funded bodies 2001-2002 (performance directors, key coaches and staff): 19% / 81%

British Universities Sports Association (BUSA officers, athletic union presidents, executive board and committee members): 39% / 61%

Institute of Leisure and Amenity Management (chief leisure officers): 12% / 88%

Female / Male

Percentage

Source: The Women's Sports Foundation UK

- it demonstrates leadership, innovation and risk-taking (an organisation at the leading edge!)
- it widens the pool of participants: this increases participation rates and, in turn, leads to a wider pool of talent to draw on for success.

Working for change in sports organisations – how can we achieve gender equity?

- Build a case for women's sport (that defines the issues in factual terms) with irrefutable evidence and rational arguments for change.
- Translate these facts into a compelling argument that tells the story of why women and girls should have more opportunities to participate and lead in sport.
- Communicate the case to those who can influence change – political leaders, regional decision-makers, chief leisure officers and governing bodies.
- Provide advanced information so that others have a chance to think about your points.
- Work with individuals from other organisations committed to gender equity both in and out of sport.
- Consult with women and girls so that you understand the barriers that prevent them from participating in or advancing in sport.

Frequently asked questions about gender equity

Question: What is gender equity all about?

Answer: Equity is concerned with correcting inequitable situations that stem from past practices. Equity means allocating resources and providing opportunities fairly and without bias or discrimination and could mean discriminating in favour of girls, for example by allocating funds to address under-participation.

The combination of cultural norms, discriminatory practice and women's position in society result in girls and women participating less in sport – although not usually by choice

---

Question: Don't girls and women choose to participate less in sport? Aren't they less interested?

Answer: Female athletes and coaches do not prefer less recognition, less power, less money and fewer choices than their male counterparts. The combination of cultural norms,

discriminatory practice and women's position in society result in girls and women participating less in sport – although not usually by choice. There is no evidence that women and girls do not like sport and in other countries there is no difference between male and female participation and achievement.

Question: Isn't the whole issue of gender equity irrelevant to many sports, in particular the single-sex sports?

Answer: Whether a sport has only female or male players, people of the opposite gender may become coaches, administrators and officials. That is why the principles of equal opportunities are relevant to all sports. A sport can maximise its human resources by recruiting from 100% of the population.

Question: Aren't gender equity programmes illegal?

Answer: Removal of barriers and traditions that deter the full participation of women and girls is necessary to give them a reasonable chance to pursue sport in any capacity. Introducing actions designed specifically for women and girls is necessary to level the playing field. Organisations that support the diverse needs of women in the short term may create the possibility of equity in the long term, benefiting those organisations and society as a whole.

- The above information is re-printed with kind permission from the Women's Sports Foundation. Visit www.wsf.org.uk for more.

© *Women's Sports Foundation*

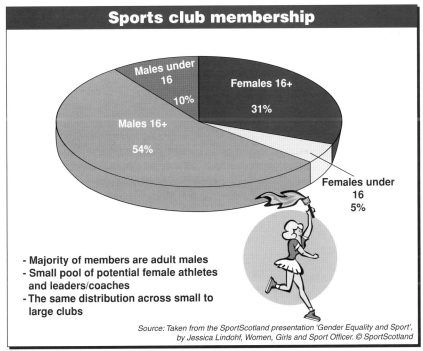

Sports club membership

Males under 16
10%

Females 16+
31%

Males 16+
54%

Females under 16
5%

- Majority of members are adult males
- Small pool of potential female athletes and leaders/coaches
- The same distribution across small to large clubs

Source: Taken from the SportScotland presentation 'Gender Equality and Sport', by Jessica Lindohf, Women, Girls and Sport Officer. © SportScotland

Facts, trends and statistics

Facts and figures about women and girls in sport

Levels of participation

Fact: Girls aged 7-11 are less than half as likely to take part in physical education and sport compared to boys (*British Medical Journal 2001*).

- Girls and young women need access to quality coaching and participation opportunities if they are to fulfil their potential.

Fact: By the age of 18, 40% of girls have dropped out of sport and physical recreation (*Youth Sport Trust 2000*).

- Quality experiences of physical education are crucial in influencing girls' continued involvement in sport and motivating them to lead active lifestyles.

By the age of 18, 40% of girls have dropped out of sport and physical recreation

---

Fact: Women are 32% less likely to participate in sport compared to men (*General Household Survey 1996; Sport England, Sports Equity Index 2001*).

- Increasing the number of women participating at every level of sport will not only widen the pool of talent available, but will also increase sports club membership, have a positive impact on the health of the nation and generally contribute to the long-term aims of social inclusion policy.

Health implications

Fact: One in three girls aged 11 in the UK is overweight and, between the ages of 16 and 24, women are twice as likely as men to be obese (*YWCA 2001*).

- Investment in sport and physical recreation will contribute to healthier lifestyles and reduce the cost of health care for obesity-related conditions.

womenssports foundation uk

Fact: One in three women over 50 has osteoporosis (*National Osteoporosis Society 2002*).

- Physical activity throughout life, particularly during the developing years, will significantly increase bone mass and help prevent osteoporosis.

Performance and excellence factors

Fact: 40% of the British Olympic team at the 2000 Olympic Games were women: they then went on to win 42% of the medals (*Women's Sports Foundation 2001*).

- Other nations have successfully demonstrated that an investment in women as athletes can reap benefits in the medals table.

Fact: Evidence from the Commonwealth Games in Manchester in 2002 demonstrates that equitable investment in women's sport could have put Britain level first in the medal tables (*Women's Sports Foundation 2002*).

- Our elite athletes deserve better: they need investment to enable them to compete as equals in the international sports arena.

Fact: Elite female athletes are just as likely as male athletes to receive income from prize money, appearance money and sponsorship, but such income is typically half that paid to male athletes (*BOA Athletes' Commission 2000*).

- The value of women's sport is still perceived as less by the media, potential sponsors and some event organisers.

Leadership

Fact: Only 8% of British Olympic team coaches at the Sydney Games in 2000 were women (*Women's Sports Foundation 2001*).

- This figure has fallen since the Atlanta Games in 1996 when 11% of coaches were female.

Fact: Only one of the 25 Olympic team managers in Sydney 2000 was a woman (*Women's Sports Foundation 2001*).

- There are insufficient numbers of female coaches, particularly at high performance levels.

Fact: 42% of sports development officers are female but women represent only 11% of principals or directors of leisure in the UK (*Institute of Leisure and Amenity Management 1999*).

- Strong leadership is a key factor in community development. Women have an important role to play in ensuring that all sectors of the community can benefit from sport.

Fact: At the 2002 Commonwealth Games, only 13% of coaches in the England team were female (*Women's Sports Foundation, 2002*).

- Special measures are needed to recruit and retain women within coaching and provide a supportive environment in which they can continue to develop and achieve the highest levels of performance.

- The above information is reprinted with kind permission from the Women's Sports Foundation. Visit www.wsf.org.uk for more information.

© WSF

Women, sport and the media

Facts and figures about women and girls in sport

The under-representation of sportswomen in all forms of media, together with the under-representation of women involved in the production of sport-related media, has long been of concern to those trying to increase the visibility of women's sport.

Visibility – how often do we see coverage of women's sport in the media?

- Most of what we know about sport we learn from the media.
- Television, radio and the print media play a central role in informing our knowledge, opinions and attitudes about women and sport.
- The media can play an important role in raising the public profile of women's sport.
- The major terrestrial and satellite television channels prioritise men's sport over women's sport.
- On satellite television the top sport shown by Sky and Eurosport is men's football while on terrestrial television men's football and men's cricket dominate.
- Television coverage of women's sport makes up only between 0.5% and 6% of all sports coverage (*Sports Council 1993*).
- Coverage of women's sport rarely shows action shots: instead, details of sportswomen's personal lives are often included inappropriately.
- Even at the start of the 21st century it is quite usual to open the sports pages of national newspapers and not find any coverage of any women's sport in the sports sections (which often extend up to 14 pages of coverage).
- Increased representation of sportswomen by the media requires increased involvement of women in the production of the media, for example producers, photographers and presenters.
- Women are under-represented in all aspects of sports news production including sports journalism, sports photography, and sports broadcasting and presenting.

Visibility – how often do we see our top sportswomen?

- Evidence shows that the visibility of women's sport is far less than men's, and fewer sports are covered.
- Public knowledge, perceptions and attitudes about women and sport are dictated by what is shown in newspapers and other forms of the media.

Television coverage of women's sport makes up only between 0.5% and 6% of all sports coverage

---

- An athlete's profile may reflect her image rather than her history within a particular sport, paying less attention to her athleticism, skill and achievements. This, in turn, undermines the status of women in sport.
- The number and diversity of role models for sportswomen and potential sportswomen are fewer.

- Sponsorship associated with women in sport is lower because women's sport receives less media coverage. However, a recent survey by the Sports Sponsorship Advisory Service reported that sponsors felt that women's sport would attract increasing attention within the next five to 10 years.

Newspaper surveys: research findings

The Women's Sports Foundation monitored five national tabloid newspapers for six weeks between December 2000 and January 2001. The amount of press coverage given to women and men was monitored and compared, and showed the following results:

- 49 issues of various newspapers were reviewed
- the newspapers reviewed had 701 pages of sports reports
- there were 1,564 photographs of men compared to 36 for women
- this accounts for just 2.3% coverage for women.

In addition, research shows that over the period of the 2002 Commonwealth Games women's sport received an average of 32% and 26% coverage in broadsheet and tabloid newspapers respectively.

It should be noted that these two surveys were carried out at different times of the year, with one focusing on a major event hosted by England. These factors will have influenced the findings.

Frequently asked questions about women, sport and the media

Question: What is the harm in portraying female athletes as pretty and feminine?
Answer: Images are powerful tools that shape and reflect attitudes and values. By portraying sportswomen

either as sex objects or only as 'pretty ladies', the message is that sportswomen are not strong, powerful and highly skilled individuals. Ultimately, images that ignore or trivialise females undermine the importance of women's sport and respect for the abilities of female athletes.

Question: So what would you have the media do? What kind of images would make women athletes happy?

Answer: The media should simply reflect the reality of women's diverse sports experiences – from grace and beauty to physical strength, endurance and power. A balanced and realistic view is what is absent in the media. Young girls and women of all ages, races and social classes are breaking down historical barriers to their participation – and this deserves to be celebrated.

A final word: big improvements... but a long way to go

Women athletes are no different from men athletes in the skill, dedication and courage they bring to their sports. There is no doubt that over the past few years there have been big improvements in the coverage of women's sport and the types of images shown, but we still have a long way to go especially in the sports pages of national newspapers.

- The above information is reprinted with kind permission from the Women's Sports Foundation. Visit www.wsf.org.uk for more information.

© WSF

A level playing field

A new national campaign has been launched celebrating the opportunities for people with disabilities to be actively involved in football

The initiative, 'A Level Playing Field', has been designed by the football authorities to highlight and promote the opportunities for disabled people to play and watch the game.

A series of events will be run until the end of the season by the Football Association, FA Premier League, Football Conference, Football Foundation and the National Association of Disabled Supporters. Highlights include:

- The campaign being profiled at England games against Northern Ireland and Azerbaijan, with Trevor Brooking presenting Level 1 coaching certificates to twenty kids from South London with Learning Difficulties at half-time at St James' Park.
- A series of events being staged at FA Premier League Clubs as part of their ongoing work to promote inclusion for disabled supporters and players.

Sir Trevor Brooking, Director of Football Development at the Football Association, said: 'We are delighted to be working in partnership with the National Association of Disabled Supporters on this unique initiative to celebrate

opportunities for disabled people in football.

'From England matches to grassroots football, we want to use this project to promote inclusion in football.'

Dave Richards, Chairman of the Premier League and Football Foundation, added: 'Since the start of the Premier League in 1992 there has been enormous investment in improving access and facilities for disabled football supporters.

'In addition, the work of the Football Foundation has helped ensure there are more opportunities than ever before for people of all ages and abilities to participate in football on a regular basis. The Football Foundation has already supported disability projects worth almost £4 million encompassing a wide range of initiatives.'

Phil Downs, Chair of the National Association of Disabled Supporters, said: 'NADS is absolutely delighted to see the Level Playing Field campaign taking off with the support of the football authorities. We hope the campaign will highlight many issues relating to disabled supporters as well as promoting the excellent community initiatives run by Clubs.

'Ultimately we hope that the match day experience will be the same for the disabled supporter as for the non-disabled supporter, and the new facilities at many of our top Clubs are enabling this to happen.'

Chris Coleman, Manager of Fulham Football Club, who today launched Fulham's first ever disabled supporters' mini-bus service, added: 'I am truly pleased that this bus will help fans who have previously been unable to travel to get to away games, and I look forward to hearing their voices cheering on the boys at Old Trafford, and all the other Premiership grounds for many games in the future.'
5 April 2005

- The above information is reprinted with kind permission from the Football Association. Visit www.thefa.com for more information.

© FA

History of drugs in sport

Introduction

The use of drugs in an attempt to enhance sporting performance is known as doping. The word 'dope' originated in South Africa. Dope referred to a primitive alcoholic drink that was used as a stimulant in ceremonial dances. Gradually the term adopted a wider usage and in reference to sport, it became known as 'doping'. In today's sporting context, doping refers to the use by athletes of prohibited substances or methods that may enhance performance.

While the term 'doping' first appeared in an English dictionary in 1879, the use of drugs is evident throughout the history of sport.

Early games

By 800BC the Greeks had incorporated sport into their lifestyles to a similar extent as the cultural and religious observations of the time. Athletic festivals were common in the Greek calendar. Emphasis was placed on the artistic nature of athletics as well as the preparatory role athletics played for warriors. Participants were required to write poetry, or perhaps display another artistic ability, as well as perform physical feats.

Athletic celebrations of this time were also an important means of establishing the geographic, economic and political importance of an area or region.

From about 400BC sport achieved a status in the social life of Greece similar to, if not greater than, its place in society today. Mass spectator sport was the order of the day and rich prizes for winners led to the emergence of a class of highly paid sports people, resulting in the demise of the amateur competitor.

Writings from the time of Plato reveal that the value of a victory in the ancient Olympics was the equivalent of nearly half a million dollars. This was complemented by other rewards including food, homes, tax exemptions and even deferment from the armed services.

Professionalism and commercialism ultimately led to corruption. Bribing and cheating became commonplace, and competitors of this period were reputedly willing to ingest any preparation which might enhance their performance, including extracts of mushrooms and plant seeds.

Roman period

The increased status of sport and the elevated position of athletes continued into the Roman period. However, the Romans adopted different sporting activities to the Greeks.

Many Roman gladiators were 'doped-up' to make their fights sufficiently vigorous and bloody for the paying public

---

Spectatorship thrived at gladiatorial competitions and chariot races, and these sporting events reigned as a source of public entertainment. To accommodate the huge following, the Coliseum was restructured in AD100 to hold 60,000 spectators.

The use of drugs during this period has also been recorded. Chariot racers fed their horses a potent mixture to make them run faster, while many gladiators were 'doped-up' to make their fights sufficiently vigorous and bloody for the paying public.

Christian era

The onset of the Christian era signalled the demise of these early games. The blood-letting nature of many of the Roman 'sports' was unacceptable to the new order of society. Eventually in AD396 the Emperor Theodosius called an end to the ancient games with a rule banning all forms of 'pagan' sports.

While sports such as wrestling and boxing were initially promoted as substitutes for the disfavoured Roman activities, these were not widely accepted and their popularity as a form of sport subsided.

Furthermore, the ethos that physical development hindered intellectual development was widely encouraged and accepted.

It was not until the nineteenth century that sport re-emerged. The impetus for this resurgence occurred in rural England and quickly spread throughout the rest of the world.

Sport in the early nineteenth century

Sport in the English society of the early nineteenth century was comprised largely of unstructured recreational activities. England was an agricultural and rural-based society and displayed forms of physical activity that were casual, communal and regionalised in nature. The type of recreational activity mirrored the pace of society.

Celebrations in respect of the harvest, or religious holidays such as Christmas, would bring the village together for a central form of entertainment. Typical celebrations consisted of:

- drinking and dancing
- games such as sack races, leapfrog and pig chasing
- activities like cockfighting and boxing matches
- football games with over 1,000 players on a field several miles long.

The onset of industrialisation and urbanisation transformed the pattern of these rural games.

Sport and the Industrial Revolution

By the latter part of the nineteenth century the rural nature of sport had given way to the influences of industrialisation and urbanisation. More organised and sophisticated forms of sporting activity emerged.

The reason for changes to traditional forms of sport can be found in wider developments in the structure and organisation of society during this period. A number of factors influenced society during the Industrial Revolution. Major changes occurred in:

Technology

The invention of new machines and manufacturing processes was the catalyst of industrialisation and urbanisation. The city became the centre of production, and following the mechanisation of many rural activities, people flocked to the cities in the search for employment.

Communication

Greater communication between people and places was required by this more sophisticated society. New forms of communication emerged such as telegraph, penny post, the newspaper and the telephone.

Transportation

Developments in transportation provided better means by which to distribute goods and services to the industrialised society. The emergence of canals, railroads and steamships also aided communication. Prior to the Industrial Revolution, travel was only undertaken for important matters. Improved methods of transportation meant that people were able to travel more freely.

Lifestyle

People moving to the cities in search of employment had to adapt from the slow-paced regional lifestyle to the quicker, more regimented living required of an urban-based population. The concept of time also became important during this period. Industrialisation brought a clear distinction between work and leisure time.

Political, economic and social structure

These factors influenced lifestyle but also contributed individually to developing the society of this period. New economic and social concerns associated with the industrial society emerged, while the power of government and an emerging middle class were important factors shaping the new society.

Influence on sport

The new urban-based population of the late nineteenth century established restricted, controlled games and activities that reflected the new regulated society. Football games played by thousands of players on a field with no boundaries were not appropriate in the city centres.

A number of developments occurred that changed the format of traditional activities. These included:

- restrictions of time and space
- formation of clubs and organised competitions
- restriction on the number of players
- development of rules

- standardisation and modification of equipment.

As the old forms of activities were modified, new sports such as rugby union, roller skating and ten-pin bowling emerged, while activities like animal baiting and cockfighting lost popularity and were eventually banned.

The Industrial Revolution had a significant impact on all aspects of sport and recreation. Technology was used to develop new equipment in sports such as golf, tennis and cricket. Other inventions also had a major impact, for example, the electric light which permitted the playing of games at night.

Improved communications enabled sports news to be despatched along cable and telephone lines, and developments in transportation allowed for inter-town and eventually international competition. These factors led to increased participation in sporting and recreational activities and significantly contributed to spreading interest in sporting activity world-wide.

Two significant outcomes of the increased involvement and interest in sport were commercialism and professionalism. Mass spectator sport replaced the communal festival and religious celebrations of earlier times.

Crowds at major soccer matches grew from a few thousand during the middle of the nineteenth century to over 100,000 by the early 1900s. Sporting facilities such as major stadiums were built and sporting events received greater coverage in newspapers and specialist magazines.

Soon the professional sportsperson took a place in society. Sport was no longer a frivolous activity to be played solely in free time. Sport, for some, now became a profession.

Sport and the twentieth century

By the turn of the century, sport was reassuming a place similar to that which it held in Greek and Roman societies. Further advances in technology combined with social, economic and political developments influenced sports development during the twentieth century.

During the twentieth century, sporting activity has gradually evolved into a 'big business' providing a significant, world-wide source of entertainment, revenue and employment.

Sport has also developed into a significant social institution and to succeed in sport has become highly valued. This has placed pressure on sportspeople to become not only successful, but the best. This pressure has contributed to the escalation in the incidence of drug taking and the number of drug-related deaths within the sporting community.

A history of international anti-doping initiatives

Prior to the implementation of drug-testing programmes in the late 1960s, the use of performance-enhancing substances by athletes appeared to be commonly accepted within the international sporting community. Athletes, coaches and administrators usually turned a blind eye to the proceedings or simply joined in.

> **In 1999 the World Anti-Doping Agency (WADA) was established as a direct result of the 1998 Tour de France doping scandal**

While drug use was reportedly rife at the 1952 Helsinki Games, and to a lesser extent at the 1956 Melbourne Olympics, countries eventually began to speak out against the harm that drugs were causing to the individual and sport.

The first significant international anti-doping development occurred in 1960 when the Council of Europe, a group of twenty-one western European nations, tabled a resolution against the use of doping substances in sport. The tide was beginning to change, from one of acceptance of doping, to a more positive anti-doping outlook.

France enacted national anti-doping legislation in 1963, leading the way for Belgium to follow the same path in 1965. The impact of anti-doping programmes, until this time, was relatively small. It

wasn't until the televised death of cyclist Tommy Simpson in the Tour de France in 1967 that the International Olympic Committee (IOC) became actively involved in international anti-doping initiatives. The Medical Commission of the IOC was established in 1967 and the first drug tests were conducted at the Mexico Games in 1968. A schedule of prohibited substances was developed by the IOC – a schedule that now includes stimulants, beta-blockers, narcotic analgesics, diuretics, anabolic agents, peptide and glycoprotein hormones, and analogues. Doping practices such as blood doping and pharmacological, chemical and physical manipulation are also prohibited.

Governments and international and national sporting organisations continued to implement anti-doping initiatives throughout the late 1960s and 1970s. Drug testing became a more common feature of high-level sporting competition.

Unfortunately, the simple fact that testing programmes were in operation did not guarantee their effectiveness. Not only were positive drug tests limited because of inadequate technology, but athletes learnt quickly how to beat the system. This included attempts to substitute urine samples and to cease using drugs in sufficient time for any trace of the drug to clear from the body prior to the drug test being taken.

In 1983, drug testing strategies took an important step forward when analytical procedures were significantly refined. The introduction of gas chromatography and mass spectrometry allowed accurate results to be consistently obtained. Also in

1983, this new technology resulted in the now famous scandal of the Pan American Games in Caracas where numerous athletes tested positive to prohibited drugs and many others left the Games without competing rather than being caught.

In 1999 the World Anti-Doping Agency (WADA) was established as a direct result of the 1998 Tour de France doping scandal.

The Tour de France scandal highlighted the need for an independent international agency, which would set unified standards for anti-doping work and co-ordinate the efforts of sports organisations and public authorities.

Following the proposal of the 1999 World Conference on Doping in Sport Conference, the World Anti-Doping Agency (WADA) was established in Lausanne on 10 November 1999. WADA is comprised of equal representation from the Olympic Movement and international government authorities. WADA moved its headquarters to Montreal, Canada in 2001.

■ Information from the Australian Sports Anti-Doping Authority. Visit www.asada.gov.au for more information.

© *Australian Government*

TO34677

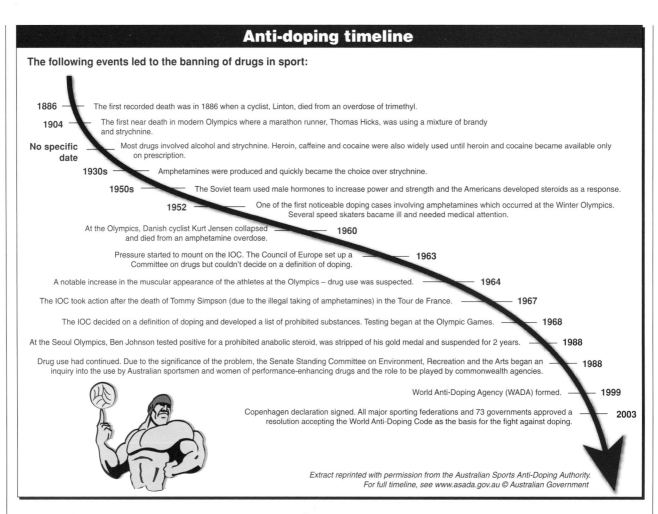

Anti-doping timeline

The following events led to the banning of drugs in sport:

1886 — The first recorded death was in 1886 when a cyclist, Linton, died from an overdose of trimethyl.

1904 — The first near death in modern Olympics where a marathon runner, Thomas Hicks, was using a mixture of brandy and strychnine.

No specific date — Most drugs involved alcohol and strychnine. Heroin, caffeine and cocaine were also widely used until heroin and cocaine became available only on prescription.

1930s — Amphetamines were produced and quickly became the choice over strychnine.

1950s — The Soviet team used male hormones to increase power and strength and the Americans developed steroids as a response.

1952 — One of the first noticeable doping cases involving amphetamines which occurred at the Winter Olympics. Several speed skaters bacame ill and needed medical attention.

At the Olympics, Danish cyclist Kurt Jensen collapsed and died from an amphetamine overdose. — **1960**

Pressure started to mount on the IOC. The Council of Europe set up a Committee on drugs but couldn't decide on a definition of doping. — **1963**

A notable increase in the muscular appearance of the athletes at the Olympics – drug use was suspected. — **1964**

The IOC took action after the death of Tommy Simpson (due to the illegal taking of amphetamines) in the Tour de France. — **1967**

The IOC decided on a definition of doping and developed a list of prohibited substances. Testing began at the Olympic Games. — **1968**

At the Seoul Olympics, Ben Johnson tested positive for a prohibited anabolic steroid, was stripped of his gold medal and suspended for 2 years. — **1988**

Drug use had continued. Due to the significance of the problem, the Senate Standing Committee on Environment, Recreation and the Arts began an inquiry into the use by Australian sportsmen and women of performance-enhancing drugs and the role to be played by commonwealth agencies. — **1988**

World Anti-Doping Agency (WADA) formed. — **1999**

Copenhagen declaration signed. All major sporting federations and 73 governments approved a resolution accepting the World Anti-Doping Code as the basis for the fight against doping. — **2003**

Extract reprinted with permission from the Australian Sports Anti-Doping Authority. For full timeline, see www.asada.gov.au © Australian Government

Drug-free sport

Information from the Department for Culture, Media and Sport

The Government is fully committed to eradicating the use of drugs and doping methods in sport. The use of performance-enhancing drugs substances and methods is cheating, unfair and contrary to the spirit of fair competition.

	2003/04	2004/05	2005/06
Self-generated income	£601,000	£685,000	£700,000
Exchequer Funding	£1.304 million	£1.715 million	£3.200 million
Total	£1.905 million	£2.400 million	£3.900 million

National anti-doping policy

National Anti-Doping Organisations are domestic organisations responsible for the planning, collection and management of anti-doping controls in their country. UK Sport is the country's National Anti-Doping Organisation (NADO). As part of its overall sporting excellence remit, UK Sport is committed to promoting ethically fair and drug-free sport, with the aim of producing sportsmen and women who are competing and winning fairly without using performance-enhancing substances.

UK Sport receives Government funding to undertake a programme of action to combat the use of drugs in sport. This includes:

- In-competition and out-of-competition testing of athletes.
- The development of a national policy framework.
- Provision of education and information services for athletes and sports governing bodies (including the Drug Information Database).

Over the previous 3 years UK Sport's Drug Free Sport Budget has been as follows:

Drug-free sport education programmes

UK Sport is also responsible for co-ordinating the UK's education programmes to British athletes and their support personnel with a number of services and resources to help them make the right decisions about what substances they can and cannot use.

100% ME is the name of UK Sport's new drug-free education programme launched on 25 May.

The programme has been developed to provide current and future sportsmen and women with the information, support, commitment and confidence to perform to the best of their ability without the use of performance-enhancing drugs. The three main elements of the campaign are:

- Outreach – promotes drug-free sport through direct interaction with athletes at events, training camps, schools and workshops.
- Tutor training – building a list of accredited advisers who can deliver advice to athletes/young people.
- Ambassadors – current and retired sportspeople will help deliver key messages and reinforce role models by influencing good behaviour in young people.

International anti-doping policy

The World Anti-Doping Agency (WADA) was established in 1999 to provide an international context for anti-doping. Its mission is to promote and coordinate, internationally, the fight against doping in sport.

A major feature of WADA's work is the World Anti-Doping Code. The Code is an international set of rules and guidelines created to protect sport from doping.

The Code will ensure that each country's drug-free sport programme at the national and international level is unified, fair and effective in regard to detection, deterrence and prevention of doping. The Code aims to simplify the anti-doping rules across all sports and countries.

Role of WADA

Its four key activity areas are the World Anti-Doping Code, Education, Research and Capacity Building.

Some of the core principles obtained in the Code include:

- Strict liability – an athlete is held responsible if a banned substance is found in their body, no matter how it got there.
- A single list of banned substances which captures the substances that are prohibited in particular sports.
- Samples can only be analysed at laboratories accredited by WADA.

- Standardisation of sanctions.
- Athletes have fundamental right to a fair hearing.

In some cases, athletes can apply for a therapeutic use exemption that gives them permission to compete with medically prescribed substances in their bodies.

In some cases, athletes can apply for a therapeutic use exemption that gives them permission to compete with medically prescribed substances in their bodies

---

A key component of the WADA Code is the List of Prohibited Substances and Methods. The list outlines those substances, their markers and doping methods that are prohibited for all athletes. The list also outlines those substances that are prohibited by certain sports.

The UK fully supports WADA and the World Anti-Doping Code.

The UNESCO Convention

A global reach on anti-doping is needed if doping is to be universally eradicated from sport. A significant development was made with the Copenhagen Declaration on Anti-Doping in Sport (March 2003), to which the UK was one of the first signatories. The declaration is essentially a memorandum of understanding that outlines governmental support for WADA and its Code.

The Copenhagen Declaration was intended as a temporary measure to unite governments to recognise the Code and support the work of WADA until such time as a legally binding convention could be developed, ratified and entered into force.

This led to the development of the UNESCO International Convention against Doping in Sport being made available to State Parties in March 2005. The Convention is a major step forward as it imposes a legal obligation on all governments to eradicate doping in sport.

The broad aims of the UNESCO Convention are to:

- Set out governments' responsibilities in the fight against doping in sport within an international legally binding document.
- Help governments give recognition to the existence and work of WADA and fulfil their obligations and contribute to WADA's operational budget.
- Act as a vehicle for governments to adopt the WADA Code and ensure that drug-free sport programmes are harmonised at international and national level.

The timescale going forwards is for interested parties to be consulted from May to August 2005. The Convention will be presented for signature at the UNESCO General Conference in October 2005. Governments are then expected to ratify the Convention in time for the Turin Winter Games in February 2006.

Nutritional supplements

The potential for sports preparations and nutritional supplements containing prohibited ingredients or being contaminated during the manufacturing process may result in an athlete receiving a full sanction even if a supplement is the source of the ingested prohibited substance.

At present no guarantee can be given that any particular supplement including vitamins and minerals, ergogenic aids (caffeine-based products) and herbal remedies are free from prohibited substances, as these products are not licensed and are not subject to the same strict manufacturing and labelling requirements as licensed medicine.

WADA and UK Sport have strongly advised athletes and sports bodies to be extremely cautious about the use of any supplements and suggest that athletes focus on eating a balanced diet, taking adequate rest and proper training.

UK Sport is currently developing a draft standard and is consulting internally and with a group of experts. They have arranged for a meeting with nutrition experts to identify the supplements that athletes are likely to need in high performance sport. This will include:

- A standard that allows athletes to identify if a manufacturer is producing a low-risk product.
- A full education programme explaining when and why supplements may be needed and alternative foods to taking supplements.
- A list of supplements that may be needed in high performance sport as recommended by a panel of experts based on scientific literature.

Success of UK's drug-free sport programme

The UK's national anti-doping programme has been hugely successful. UK Sport has carried out over 29,000 doping tests across more than 40 sports in the last 5 years (1999-2004). Of these, 431 showed adverse findings representing just 1.5% of all tests, which is significantly better than the global average of 2% for this period. This suggests that the UK's drug-testing programme is an effective deterrent in the fight against doping in sport. This suggests that UK's drug testing programme is an effective deterrent in the fight against doping in sport.

In 2003, the UK had less than 1% adverse drugs test findings (72 adverse findings from 7,618 tests) compared to the global average of 1.62%

WADA's latest statistics for 2003 show that the UK's results compare favourably with other parts of the world. In 2003, the UK had less than 1% adverse findings (72 adverse findings from 7,618 tests) compared to the global average of 1.62%. This suggests that our programme is extremely competent and is discouraging British athletes to cheat.

- Information from the Department for Culture, Media and Sport. Visit www.culture.gov.uk for more.

© Crown copyright

Why athletes take drugs

Information from the Australian Sports Anti-Doping Authority

Why do athletes use drugs?

There are a number of factors that may contribute to an athlete misusing drugs. These factors can be related to the drug, the athlete or the athlete's environment.

Drug
- effects of the drug
- ease of availability
- legal status
- physical dependence.

Person
- dissatisfaction with performance and progress
- psychological dependence
- desire to cope with anxiety or stress
- desire to relax / socialise

- values – using drugs may not be considered a problem
- belief that others are using drugs
- temptation to think they can get away with it
- problem of being easily influenced by others
- lack of knowledge about side effects
- lack of confidence.

Environment
- friends or other athletes using drugs
- culture of the sport
- pressure to win from coach, parents, public, media
- financial reward
- prestige and fame

- advertising
- influence of role models
- unrealistic qualifying standards or performance expectations
- national pride.

Specific pressures

Self

The basic desire to be successful and satisfy ego requirements is a major source of internal pressure. Problems such as self-doubt, lack of confidence, nervousness, stress and depression are common to all athletes. The characteristics of self-pressure are not exclusive to people in the sporting field.

Coach

A successful athlete is often associated with a successful coach. As a result, the coach may place direct pressure on an athlete to perform and may be the source of further internal pressure.

Peer

Competitors set the standards to which an athlete must perform. If an athlete believes that a competitor has obtained some kind of advantage, then the pressure to also have or use this advantage is significant, for example, a better-designed golf club, a lighter running shoe or the use of steroids. Similar peer-group pressure may come from team-mates.

Family

The expectations of family and friends are often a source of pressure, particularly at the lower levels of competition. Previously successful family members may also create pressure.

Spectators/crowd

Spectators create a great source of pressure both at the elite and lower levels of competition. At the elite level, athletes are often adopted as role models and will often take the hopes and aspirations of thousands of fans into competition.

Spectators are also the source of money and applause, hence the athlete may feel pressure to perform to standards expected by the public. The fickle nature of public support also creates pressure. Generally, we all love a winner and often adopt a 'win at all costs' mentality.

At the lower level of competition the presence of spectators may increase the anxiety levels of athletes. This may affect an athlete's performance and in due course influence an athlete's behaviour.

Media

The media play an important role in shaping the opinions and attitudes of the general public. How the media portray an athlete, and how they report on an athlete's performance, can not only influence the public but the athlete as well.

Administrators/promoters

Unreasonable scheduling of competitions and the establishment of unrealistic performance standards are ways in which sports administrators may contribute to the pressures on athletes. Similarly, promoters of sports events usually demand a high standard of performance from athletes to enhance the credibility and the promotional qualities of events they sponsor.

Social

Pressure for sporting success may also be the result of social incentives to achieve. The glory and recognition for sporting achievements is a strong motivator towards success. Sporting success may provide an athlete with greater access and mobility to other social groups, that is, successful athletes are usually given the opportunity to meet and mix with people outside their usual social group, such as politicians and media personalities.

The fickle nature of public support creates pressure. Generally, we all love a winner and often adopt a 'win at all costs' mentality

---

Financial and material rewards

Financial and material rewards are major influences on athletes and sporting performance. Sport, which was once an activity to fill in leisure time, has now become a way to earn a living for some of our elite athletes. In recent times people have commented that money-making principles have begun to replace athletes' moral principles.

Enormous salaries, product endorsements and potential careers outside of the sporting field are some of. the rewards available to the successful athlete. Rewards are also available to athletes at lower levels of competition and to those in amateur sport. Even at junior levels, inducements such as scholarships are a significant incentive, and can increase the pressure to achieve.

National/political/ideological

Successful athletes at the highest level are sometimes elevated to the position of hero and carry the pressures of national honour and pride with them. Countries also use their athletes as political weapons. In international competition, one country's sporting successes over another country are often viewed as proof of ideological or national superiority. Such is the case in the Olympic Games, where enormous emphasis is placed on the number of gold medals won by a country, with even greater pressure being placed on the host country.

Factors such as an athlete's desire to win, the desire to please their coach and family, the glory of victory and the social and economic reward of sporting success often send the athlete in search of a competitive edge. Sometimes this search leads to the use of drugs.

■ The above information is reprinted with kind permission from the Australian Sports Anti-Doping Authority. Visit www.asada.gov.au for more information.

© *Australian Government*

Testing time as anti-doping laws get tougher

By Simon Hart

Britain's leading sportsmen and women will have to nominate one hour every day, five days a week, when they will be available for out-of-competition drug-testing to clamp down on athletes who suddenly go missing when the testers call. Athletes who miss three tests within 18 months will face a two-year ban.

The crackdown is part of a new set of anti-doping rules being published by UK Sport tomorrow that will bring the country's sporting governing bodies into line with the World Anti-Doping Code. Sports will have to adopt the new measures as a condition of receiving public funding.

Under the old rules, if an athlete was absent when a drug-testing team arrived, the inspectors would make up to three attempts in a five-day period to make contact. Now, a failure to show up during the appointed hour without notifying the testers in advance will constitute a missed test – unless there are 'exceptional circumstances'.

However, a number of sports, particularly outdoor ones, have expressed reservations about the practicality of expecting athletes to set aside a specific hour of their day when training schedules are at the mercy of the weather and often subject to last-minute change.

Athletes who hold down full-time occupations may also find the new regulations unworkable. It is understood that one Olympic athlete is already contemplating retirement from international competition because his job requires him to be on 24-hour call and he cannot predict where and when he will be working.

Under the rules, athletes will be required to provide UK Sport, the Government agency responsible for drug-testing in Britain, with details of their nominated hours three months in advance, though they will be able to change their schedule via a special athletes' website or by fax. UK Sport say they will also accept a telephone call for last-minute alterations.

By putting the responsibility on the athletes, UK Sport will be hoping to avoid the confusion surrounding the case of the Greek sprinters, Kostas Kenteris and Katerina Thanou, who were recently cleared by their own athletics federation of knowingly missing three random dope tests, the last of which was at the Athens Olympics and involved their infamous midnight motorbike ride.

Athletes who miss three tests within 18 months will face a two-year ban

The pair, who still face a hearing at the Court of Arbitration for Sport, maintain they were not aware that they were required by the dope-testers. Such a defence would not be open to British athletes under the new regulations, however, because the very act of nominating an hour every day could be taken as giving permission to be tested at that time.

Although the regulations will add to the burden on sportsmen and women, the British Athletes Commission, who represent the concerns of elite athletes, have welcomed the changes. Chief executive Pete Gardner, a former rower, said: 'Most athletes train at the same venue every day so it's not that difficult to work out where you are going to be for one hour a day.

'There are some sports, particularly the outdoor sports, where it is less straightforward. If you take rowing, for example, you often get a situation where you get up in the morning and it's howling with wind and one of the courses you train on is unrowable, so the chief coach says you're going to train somewhere else.

'It's difficult for you to phone someone at seven in the morning to say you're going to be training at a different location, but I've been assured by UK Sport that they are going to be sitting down with these kinds of sports to work out a system whereby this can work. Maybe it will be left to the chief coach to notify the testers.

'Once these kinds of problems are sorted out, I actually think it will be a good thing. A lot of athletes will feel that, yes, the new system is a pain in the neck, but they will also feel that it's something that's totally necessary.'

15 May 2005

The World Anti-Doping Code

What athletes need to know

The World Anti-Doping Code is an international set of rules and guidelines devised to protect sport from doping. It aims to simplify the anti-doping rules, with a fair and comprehensive guide for athletes across the globe.

As an athlete, you are solely responsible for your own actions. If you break the anti-doping rules of sport – even unwittingly – you could face a two-year or a lifetime ban. For this reason it is vital that you understand what the Code is about and what it means to you. This fact sheet will tell you what you need to know.

Testing programme

For athletes, testing is the most effective way of demonstrating that you compete without the use of prohibited substances or methods.

The Code requires Anti-Doping Organisations, such as UK Sport and your International Federation (IF), to nominate the levels at which they plan to test. For this reason, UK Sport has established two testing pools, a National Registered Testing Pool (NRTP) and a Domestic Testing Pool (DTP).

All athletes in the DTP should submit Therapeutic Use Exemption (TUE) applications if they are prescribed a prohibited substance for a legitimate medical condition (see below for more information).

In addition, if you are in the DTP, you may also be nominated for the NRTP. This means that you will be required to provide whereabouts details to UK Sport or your IF.

How do I know which testing pool I am in?

You can find out if you are in the Domestic Testing Pool by logging on to 'Testing Pools' on the main toolbar www.didglobal.com or by contacting your sport's governing body. If you are selected for the NRTP you will be notified directly by UK Sport or your sport's governing body and you will have an opportunity to receive additional education about providing athlete whereabouts.

REMEMBER: If you are not in the NRTP or the DTP you may still be selected at random for testing so it is important that you adhere to the anti-doping rules at all times.

Violating the anti-doping rules

If you violate the anti-doping rules you are risking your sporting career and perhaps bringing your sport, country and reputation into disrepute.

The current anti-doping rule violations are:

- The presence of a prohibited substance in a specimen
- The use or attempted use of a prohibited substance/method
- Avoidance or refusal to undertake a sample collection
- Failure to provide whereabouts information
- Tampering or attempting to tamper with any part of the doping control process
- Possession or trafficking of prohibited substances/methods.

Inadvertent doping

Inadvertent doping occurs when an athlete takes a medication to treat an illness or injury – unaware that it contains a banned substance. It can also occur if an athlete takes a supplement which contains a prohibited substance. This can either be through contamination or because not all the ingredients were listed. UK Sport strongly advises athletes not to take supplements.

Under the WADC, ignorance is no excuse in such cases – you are solely responsible for checking the status of all medication and substances you use. Athletes that have unwittingly taken a prohibited substance will still face sanctions.

Prohibited list

In order to ensure that you are not unknowingly taking banned substances, it is necessary to be familiar with the most current Prohibited List (which is subject to change from time to time). This list outlines each prohibited class of substance with examples.

A current edition of the list can be found on the UK Sport Drug Information Database (DID) www.uksport.gov.uk/did or the WADA website www.wada-ama.org. You can also use DID to check the status of UK licensed medications. A new list is reissued every year on January 1, but updates may be made by WADA throughout the year so it is worth checking regularly for any changes.

To avoid testing positive for a banned substance, remember:
– Check all medications carefully against the prohibited list before use
– Inform your doctor or pharmacist about the rules under which you compete.

Therapeutic exemption forms

Sometimes you may need to take a banned substance for a legitimate medical condition. In this case you should first check with your doctor to see if there are any permitted alternative treatments or medications. If this is not possible, you will need to apply for a Therapeutic Use Exemption (TUE) using the correct application forms.

There are two types of TUE applications:

1. Abbreviated TUE (ATUE) – This is required for some inhaled asthma medications and some products containing glucocorticosteroids, like eye drops. ATUEs are considered valid on receipt of a fully and appropriately completed ATUE form by the relevant organisation – either your National Anti-Doping Organisation (UK Sport), or your International Federation if you compete internationally.
2. Standard TUE – These forms will be reviewed by a panel of independent physicians, known as a Therapeutic Use Exemption Com-mittee (TUEC). Where possible, athletes should only use a prohibited substance once

an exemption has been granted (except with acute or emergency treatments).

For further information on whether you need to apply for a TUE and where to send the application, check the TUE section of our website: www.uksport.gov.uk/did.

Sanctions

What happens if you test positive?

There is a clear and definitive set of sanctions if you are caught using banned substances. First offenders could face a two-year ban from competing in any sport which has signed the WADA code. Athletes caught a second time may be banned for life.

All athletes are entitled to a hearing before the sanction is applied. However, all relevant competition results will be automatically disqualified – regardless of the hearing outcome.

And finally, remember:
- Using drugs is cheating – you are cheating yourself and your fellow athletes.

- By taking drugs, you are risking your own health and possibly the safety of fellow competitors.
- If you do take drugs, there is a strong possibility that you will get caught.
- You could bring your reputation, your coach, your team and your country into disrepute.

Services and help lines – We are here to help

There are plenty of ways that you can access further information and advice on the World Anti-Doping Code and the anti-doping rules of your sport and UK Sport. This information is accessible to all athletes by:
- Telephone – freephone 0800 528 0004 (from 9am to 5pm, Monday to Friday).
- Email – drug-free@uksport.gov.uk
- Internet – www.didglobal.com

- The above information is reprinted with kind permission from 100%Me. Visit www.100percentme. co.uk for more information.

© UK Sport

Athletes' advice

There are many ways athletes can avoid making mistakes in anti-doping. UK Sport provides athletes with many services and resources that help athletes make their own informed choices

There are a lot of things athletes need to do to make sure they are competing drug-free, but once you know what to do and how to do it, competing drug-free is pretty easy.

You can start by asking yourself some simple questions:

1. Do you use medication without checking the label?
YES
If you don't check your medication before you use it you could be at risk of breaking the rules. You should always check the status of any substance before you use it and if you're not sure, ask UK Sport or your team doctor to help you find the answer.
DID YOU KNOW...
That many athletes have lost medals because they took a medication without checking the label. You

may remember Alain Baxter, the Winter Olympian that bought a Vicks Inhaler in the US that was banned. He thought it was the same as the UK product but it contained different ingredients. Always check the label.

2. Have you told your doctor or your pharmacist that you have to follow the anti-doping rules of sport?
NO
It is your responsibility to tell your doctor or your pharmacist that you follow anti-doping rules. You shouldn't expect them to know and you can't blame them if you take something you shouldn't have. You could give them a copy of your advice card or the Drug Information Database address at www.uksport. gov.uk/did
DID YOU KNOW...
That some athletes have been banned from sport because they took medication from a family member. More recently, Australian cricket legend Shane Warne claimed he took a fluid-reducing

tablet to help his appearance. The tablet was a prohibited substance called a Diuretic. Warne was banned from sport for 12 months.

3. Do you know your rights as an athlete in the testing programme?
NO

You should always know your rights as an athlete in the testing programme to ensure that the procedures are conducted to the international standard. You should know what to expect throughout the testing procedures and if you notice any discrepancies you should report these to UK Sport or your governing body.

DID YOU KNOW...

That if you are under the age of 18 years you have the right and are encouraged to take a representative of your choice with you to the doping control station. If you wish you may also have the representative present during sample collection.

4. Do you use supplements, for example, vitamins, mineral or herbal products?
YES

If you use supplements you may be at risk of breaking the anti-doping rules. This is because supplements are not licensed products and do not follow the same strict manufacturing and labelling requirements as licensed medicines, such as ibuprofen. This means that supplement manufacturers do not always know exactly what is in the end product because they don't necessarily produce the raw material.

DID YOU KNOW...

Many athletes have failed drugs tests because they used supplements that were contaminated with banned substances, such as the steroid nandrolone or stimulants like ephedrine. You should always try to find a permitted alternative to maintaining your health and nutrition, in particular, by establishing a balanced diet.

Advice to athletes
- Always check the status of any substance before you use it.
- Contact UK Sport if you cannot find the status of a substance.
- Be very careful when using foreign products and if you are travelling abroad avoid having to buy foreign products by taking some common permitted medication with you, for example, paracetamol, hayfever medication etc...
- Practise using the DID in the UK and abroad.
- Speak to a qualified nutritionist about your diet and avoid the use of supplements.
- Read the testing procedures and know your rights as an athlete.

- The above information is reprinted with kind permission from UK Sport. Visit www.uksport.gov.uk for more information.

© UK Sport

Drug tests in sport up 11% last year

By Russell Langley

Figures released today by UK Sport, the UK's National Anti-Doping Organisation, show that more than 6,500 drug tests were undertaken in the UK over the past year (April 2004-March 2005). The final total of 6,520 marks an 11% increase on the previous year (5,876 tests).

The figures include the 1,016 tests conducted as part of the pre-Games testing programme for Britain's Olympic and Paralympic competitors – the most comprehensive pre-Games programme ever conducted in the UK. There were no positive findings throughout this programme.

In total, 49 sports have been covered by the testing programme over the course of the year. The governing bodies receiving the most tests were: Football Association (1,516), UK Athletics (498), Rugby Football Union (340), British Swimming (338) and Rugby Football League (304).

In line with the guidelines set out by the World Anti-Doping Agency (WADA), there has been a shift towards more no-notice, out-of-competition tests, either at training sessions or other venues. These made up 50.6% of the testing programme, compared with 42.7% in 2003/04.

With information on positive findings not being released until the full disciplinary process is complete, it is not yet possible to produce a final total of findings for the year as some cases, mainly from the last quarter (January-March 2005), remain open. It does appear, however, that the percentage of findings will be lower than the worldwide average of 1.72% unveiled last week by WADA.

'The ratio of positive findings to the number of tests conducted continues to fall as it has done over the past three years,' said John Scott, Director of Drug-Free Sport

at UK Sport. 'This is encouraging, particularly in a year when such a comprehensive testing programme has been in place in our priority sports. Full details of all findings will of course be made public through our Drug Results Database as and when the cases are closed by the governing bodies concerned. Under the rules of the World Anti-Doping Code, this will include the names of the competitors.'

Approximately 7,000 tests are expected to be conducted in 2005/06 as UK Sport further increases its commitment to drug-free sport. This will include large-scale pre-Games testing programmes for both the Winter Olympics in Turin and the Commonwealth Games in Melbourne. However, Scott is keen to point out that testing is not the only weapon at UK Sport's disposal in the fight against doping in sport.

'Testing is clearly a powerful deterrent and detection tool for us, but we feel education has an equally, if not more important, role to play,' he said. 'Later this month we are launching a major new anti-doping education campaign, through which we aim to influence the attitudes and opinions towards doping of both current and future sportsmen and women. We hope this will have a long-term impact on British competitors, and help British sport maintain its standing of integrity and fairness on the world stage.'

16 May 2005

■ The above information is reprinted with kind permission from UK Sport. For more information, please visit the UK Sport website at www.uksport.gov.uk

© UK Sport

Demand for doping ban to be doubled

Some of the world's leading athletes want dope cheats to be banned for four years for a first drugs offence instead of two as presently under the rules of the World Anti-Doping Agency

Some of the world's leading athletes want dope cheats to be banned for four years for a first drugs offence instead of two as presently under the rules of the World Anti-Doping Agency.

Rania Elwani, the Egyptian swimmer who is a member of the WADA Athletic Committee, said yesterday: 'Everybody clean wants a stronger ban.'

However, her committee contains no footballers. Elwani conceded that they have to discuss the matter with

By Mihir Bose

football players, whose governing body, Fifa, feel that the existing two-year ban is too heavy for a first offence.

WADA set out their anti-doping stall with president Dick Pound saying that he did not expect gene doping to be an issue in Turin. However: 'If it does happen we can identify it,' he said.

Gene doping involves transferring genes directly into human cells to blend into an athlete's DNA, in order to enhance muscle growth and increase strength or endurance. On Jan 27 it came to light that disgraced German coach Thomas Springstein, accused of supplying drugs to minors, was being investigated for gene doping.

About 1,200 tests will be conducted in Turin, an increase of 72 per cent on the 2002 Salt Lake City Games. So far 101 doping tests have been conducted with no positive results.

Pound is sceptical that the National Hockey League players will produce positive results, despite the fact that he feels the new NHL anti-doping plan 'is full of holes. There are

no off-season tests. And you're not allowed to test a player after a game or before a game.' Hockey players who come to the Olympics, says Pound, will have had time to clear their systems of banned substances.

Gene doping involves transferring genes directly into human cells to blend into an athlete's DNA, in order to enhance muscle growth and increase strength or endurance

Pound said he welcomed the out-of-court settlement between athlete Marion Jones and Victor Conte, owner of the BALCO sports nutrition laboratory, over claims that he had supplied her with drugs. However, Pound added: 'Wearing my IOC hat, there is disappointment. Because of the settlement a lot of information around Balco will not now be available.'

10 February 2006

© Telegraph Group Limited 2006

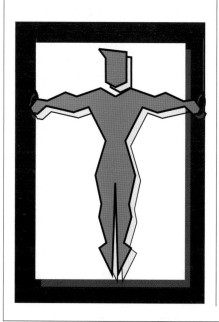

Gym drugs

Can certain substances serve as a short cut to shaping up? All the facts, right here

We're talking supplements

Anabolic steroids are often taken in a 'stack' with a number of other drugs and drug-like supplements, or the drug-like supplements may be taken on their own. The use of these supplements seems to have become more common, and in recent years the number of different products available has also increased. Some of the products mentioned below are completely legal to use and are openly sold in health food stores, but others are now considered to be potentially dangerous and their legal status is under review in several different countries. The category of 'drug-like supplements' does not include simpler nutritional supplements such as multivitamins or protein drinks.

Androstenedione (andro)

This is a chemical that is produced naturally in the human body. It's converted into testosterone and oestrogen, and may pose the same risks to health as anabolic steroids, such as damage to the heart, liver and kidneys, masculine changes in women, mood changes, and erection problems or breast growth in men.

Nandrolone precursors

A number of food supplements available as 'training aids' are now thought to contain nandrolone precursors. These are chemical substances that appear to be converted into the anabolic steroid nandrolone when eaten or drunk, and combined with strenuous exercise. If these permitted chemicals

are capable of being converted into nandrolone, then it is likely it will have the same health risks as the other anabolic steroids. There have been several cases of athletes who have tested positive for nandrolone and thrown out of competitions, but who strongly deny ever knowingly taking the banned anabolic steroid.

Nalbuphine hydrochloride (Nubaine/Nubain)

This drug is an analgesic (painkiller) that some people inject before a workout. It prevents them feeling the pain of over-exertion, which makes serious injuries much more likely. Nalbuphine also has mood altering effect, and is opiate-based like drugs such as morphine and heroin. This substance is highly addictive, and most heavy steroid users even describe it as 'a junkie's drug'.

Clenbuterol hydrochloride

Clenbuterol is medically prescribed for the treatment of asthma, but it is sometimes abused because some people think it can burn off fat and slow down the process where the body breaks down protein. Side effects include tremors (shaking), high blood pressure (hypertension), difficulty sleeping, and headaches.

Diuretics

These drugs stimulate the flow of urine, and remove fluids from the body. Bodybuilders sometimes take them before shows to counteract the fluid-retaining side effects of steroids, and to make their muscles appear larger. Unfortunately, strong diuretics also remove vital ions such as potassium along with the fluid, which can cause cramping and collapse.

Erythropoetin ('EPO')

This is an injectable synthetic hormone that stimulates the body to make more red cells. It allows the blood to carry more oxygen, theoretically increasing a person's ability to exercise, although it has never been shown to improve athletic performance. More cells in the blood make it thicker, which increases the risk of life-threatening blood clots in deep veins or the lungs, heart attacks and strokes.

Ephedrine

This is a stimulant substance that's extracted from a plant known as Ephedra or Ma Huang which is sometimes used in oriental medicine as a tonic. Ephedrine is sold legally in the United States, but is banned in the UK. It gives users an amphetamine-like rush of energy, and is sometimes taken just before a workout to give the user the drive to work harder and push themselves further physically. Side effects include seizures (fits), heart attacks, irregular heartbeat, and possibly miscarriage, or even death.

Caffeine

This naturally occurring drug is found in coffee, tea, chocolate, and colas. Large amounts of purified caffeine are added to certain 'training aids' to give an energy boost before someone starts exercising, or it might be taken in the form of caffeine pills. Some 'training aids' mix caffeine with ephedrine, and sometimes with aspirin. Taking high doses of caffeine causes sleep disturbances and a feeling of 'jitteriness' or irritability. Deaths from caffeine poisoning are rare but have been reported occasionally.

■ The above information is reprinted with kind permission from TheSite. For more information on this and other topics, please visit their website at www.thesite.org

© TheSite.org

Drugs and methods in sport – effects and risks

Using a drug to improve performance is cheating. The World Anti-Doping Agency lists all those drugs that are prohibited either because they are classed as performance enhancing, a health risk or they 'violate the spirit of sport'.

New drugs are being developed all of the time, so the list of banned substances is updated every year. To find out whether or not any particular drug is banned you can check its status on the UK Sport Drug Information Database.

Anabolic steroids

What are they?

Steroids are natural or man-made substances that act like the hormone testosterone. Both men and women have testosterone naturally in their bodies but males have more, which is why they tend to grow larger, stronger and hairier than females. Steroids stimulate the development of male sexual characteristics and the build-up of muscle tissue. They are sometimes used medically to help recovery from an operation and to treat breast cancer.

Why do some athletes use them?

Because of their effect on the build-up of muscle tissue, athletes may be tempted to use steroids in any sport where strength, speed or size is an advantage in order to increase their muscle strength and power. Athletes have been known to take steroids during training to allow them to train harder and in competition to increase their aggression and competitiveness.

What are the risks?

Steroids affect the body's natural hormonal balance and cause a range of serious side effects. Many of the side effects are permanent and do not disappear once steroid use has stopped.

Harmful effects on both males and females can include:

- increased violence, aggression, extreme mood swings and personality changes (sometimes known as 'Roid Rage')
- serious damage to the liver
- an increased risk of heart disease, kidney damage and cancer
- an increased risk of muscle injury
- adolescents may permanently stop growing.

Steroids are natural or man-made substances that act like the hormone testosterone

---

Harmful effects on males can include:

- development of breasts (these do not always disappear when the steroid use is stopped)
- hardening and shrinking of testicles and reduced sperm production
- impotence.

Harmful effects on females can include:

- development of male features such as a deep voice, facial and body hair
- stopping of menstrual periods
- changes in the sexual organs
- miscarriage or damage to the baby if steroids are used during pregnancy
- infertility.

Are they banned?

Steroids are banned both for use in and out of competition in all sports. In the UK steroids are a Class C drug which means that it is a criminal offence to produce or supply them.

Stimulants

What are they?

Stimulants are a class of drugs that act on the central nervous system in the same way as the hormone adrenalin, by speeding up parts of the brain and the body's reactions. Common street drugs that are stimulants include cocaine, amphetamines (Speed) and Ecstasy.

Caffeine in coffee, tea, chocolate and cola drinks is a stimulant and has only recently been removed from the list of banned substances.

Stimulants are also often found in cold and hay fever remedies and in herbal and nutritional substances that can be bought without a prescription. Athletes must take great care to check any medication or supplements that they take in order to avoid unknowingly taking more than an allowed level of stimulant.

Why do some athletes use them?

Stimulants can make an athlete feel more competitive and more alert. They can stop the athlete feeling tired or hungry. Athletes might use stimulants to lose weight and to help them exercise for longer.

What are the risks?

Stimulants make the heart beat faster and increase the body temperature and breathing rate. They can also cause the following harmful effects:

- overheating – this can cause the organs of the body to stop working
- difficulty sleeping
- heart problems
- sweating, shaking and anxiety
- addiction
- depression, mood swings and aggression.

Are they banned?
Most types of stimulant are prohibited in competition. Some stimulants, such as cocaine, are classified in the UK as a Class A drug and amphetamines and related substances are classified as a Class B drug (or Class A if prepared for injection), making possession and supply a criminal offence.

Diuretics

What are they?
Diuretics are a type of drug that increases the amount of urine produced and therefore reduces the amount of fluid in the body. They can help to reduce tissue swelling and are used medically to treat kidney disease and high blood pressure.

Why do some athletes use them?
Athletes who are involved in sports that have weight categories may be tempted to use diuretics to help lose weight quickly. Sports where weight loss may be an advantage include the martial arts, rowing, boxing, weight lifting and ski jumping. Athletes have also taken diuretics to speed up the rate that other banned drugs are passed out of their body.

What are the risks?
The main risk of using diuretics is dehydration.

Dehydration means that the body does not have enough water to work properly and can have the following effects:
- headaches
- feeling sick and dizzy
- heart and kidney disease
- collapse.

Are they banned?
Diuretics are banned in all sports as masking agents (to hide the effects of another prohibited substance) both in and out of competition. In some sports diuretics can be used for medical reasons with permission from a doctor. The use of diuretics is completely prohibited in and out of competition in sports where weight categories are applied.

Peptide hormones and analogues

What are they?
Hormones are chemicals that send signals to parts of the body and control certain functions. Hormones are made of peptides which are chains of amino acids. Analogues are man-made chemicals that have the same effect as a hormone.

Why do some athletes use them?
Athletes may be tempted to use a range of different hormones for a variety of reasons. In particular athletes have been known to take human Growth Hormone (hGH) to increase muscle growth and the oxygen-carrying red blood cells. This might be an advantage in endurance sports such as marathon running and cross-country skiing.

The use of additional hormones in an otherwise healthy person upsets the normal hormonal balance of the body which then attempts to redress the balance

---

Other hormones that have been used by athletes are the female pregnancy hormone chorionic gonadotrophin (hCG) which increases testosterone production and corticotrophin (ACTH) which helps repair damaged muscle and creates a feeling of wellbeing.

What are the risks?
The use of additional hormones in an otherwise healthy person upsets the normal hormonal balance of the body which then attempts to redress the balance. Excess human Growth Hormone in adults causes acromegaly. This is the abnormal and distorted growth of the hands, feet, facial feature and bodily organs. It also has other serious side effects including increased risk of diabetes and heart disease.

The use of erythropoietin (EPO) brings with it the serious dangers caused by thickening of the blood, such as the risk of blood clots, stroke and heart attack.

Are they banned?
The use of hormones and their analogues are prohibited in sport. Males only are prohibited from using the female pregnancy hormone hCG and athletes with diabetes are permitted to use insulin with permission from a doctor.

Beta-blockers

What are they?
Beta-blockers are a group of drugs used to reduce blood pressure. They work by slowing down the heart rate preventing dilation of the blood vessels. These effects reduce the workload of the heart and help to prevent heart attacks in people who have heart trouble and high blood pressure.

Beta-blockers are also known as anxiety reducing drugs.

Why do some athletes use them?
Beta-blockers reduce energy and increase fatigue and so would not improve an athlete's performance in sports requiring stamina or strength. However, they have been used by athletes competing in sports requiring control. Beta-blockers slow down the heart rate and competitors may use them to steady their hand in target sports or to reduce anxiety in sports requiring bodily movements or vehicle control.

What are the risks?
If a healthy person takes beta-blockers they run the risk of lowering their blood pressure and slowing their heart rate to dangerously low levels. Some beta-blockers have also been found to increase the chances of depression and actually to increase feelings of anxiety and tension.

Are they banned?
Beta-blockers are prohibited in competition in specified sports, particularly target sports such as archery, shooting, curling and nine-pin bowling. They are also banned in sports involving body movements such as gymnastics, ski jumping and synchronised swimming and in sports involving control of a vehicle such as bobsleigh and motor cycling.

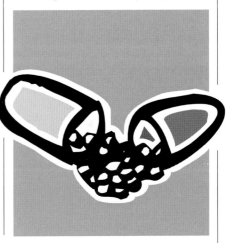

Narcotic analgesics

What are they?

Narcotic analgesics are strong painkillers made from opiates taken from the poppy plant. They work by reducing the amount of pain that is felt by the brain, and some narcotic analgesics can give the user a feeling of powerfulness and fearlessness. Well-known narcotic analgesics include diamorphine (heroin) and the milder analgesic codeine which is often used in over-the-counter remedies for colds and diarrhoea.

Why do some athletes use them?

Athletes may need to use painkillers to treat an injury. However, it may be tempting for an athlete to continue to train or compete with an injury, by using a narcotic analgesic to mask the pain. This could make the original injury worse. Athletes have also been known to use narcotic analgesics in sports such as boxing to raise their pain threshold and reduce fear.

What are the risks?

Narcotic analgesics are highly addictive and in high doses they can cause drowsiness, slow breathing, loss of concentration, coordination and balance. Overdoses can cause coma and death.

Are they banned?

Certain narcotic analgesics, such as codeine, are permitted in sport. Many others, such as heroin, are prohibited in all sports. Many narcotic analgesics are categorised as Class A drugs in the UK, meaning manufacture, supply and possession of them is a criminal offence.

Cannabinoids

What is it?

Cannabis is the most commonly used illicit drug in the UK and is made from the dried flowers, leaves or resin of the cannabis plant. The active chemical in cannabis is THC (delta-9-tetrahydrocannabinol) and this causes a series of reactions in the brain that lead to feelings of relaxation and reduced inhibition. It is also known as marijuana, hashish, cannabinoids and pot.

Why do some athletes use it?

Athletes are unlikely to use cannabis to improve their performance because of its effects of increasing drowsiness and impairing balance, coordination and concentration.

It is more likely to be used as a recreational drug. However, cannabis could possibly be used to reduce a competitor's anxiety or to steady their nerves.

What are the risks?

In small amounts, cannabis can distort perception of time and space and can impair an athlete's coordination, perception and thinking skills. It also increases the heart rate and reduces the oxygen-carrying capacity of the blood. In the first hour after taking cannabis the user's risk of a heart attack quadruples.

Long-term use of cannabis has been found to be even more dangerous than smoking tobacco. Marijuana smoke contains 50% more carcinogens (cancer-causing chemicals) than tobacco smoke and regular users are more likely to suffer from chest illnesses and breathing problems. Long-term marijuana use can lead to addiction for some users and its adverse affect on memory, attention and hearing lasts for weeks after the drug is last taken.

Is it banned?

The use of cannabis is prohibited in competition in all sports. Users should be aware that detectable traces of cannabis can remain in the bloodstream for several weeks after it is last used. In the UK, cannabis is a Class C substance meaning it is a criminal offence to produce, possess or supply it.

Blood doping

What is it?

Blood doping is a prohibited technique (not a substance). It involves removing some of the athlete's blood a few months before a competition and storing it. The athlete's blood levels return to normal over time and then about a week before competition the blood is injected back into the athlete.

Why do some athletes use it?

The technique increases the amount of red blood cells in the athlete's body, increasing their oxygen-carrying capacity. This can help to improve performance in endurance sports such as cycling and running.

What are the risks?

Blood doping can cause blood clots and overload of the blood system, as well as carrying with it the risk of introducing infectious diseases such as HIV and hepatitis.

Is it banned?

Blood doping is banned in all sports.

■ The above information is reprinted with kind permission from 100% Me, an athlete-centred anti-doping campaign from UK Sport. For more information about prohibited substances and their effects, please visit the 100% Me website at www.100percentme.co.uk.

© UK Sport

Gene therapy promises the holy grail

By Nick Morgan

A new gene therapy technique, which is more than twice as effective as steroids at boosting muscle, will soon be given the go-ahead for testing on humans. After that, doctors say, it is 'inevitable' that athletes will try to use it to enhance their performance.

The technique was developed by Professor Geoff Goldspink of the Royal Free Hospital in London to combat muscular dystrophy, a degenerative condition that affects about 30,000 people in the UK.

Professor Goldspink discovered that injected genetic material could increase production of a protein called mechano growth factor, or MGF, which boosts muscle mass and improves the muscle's ability to repair itself.

By cloning the gene and injecting it into mice, Professor Goldspink recorded an increase in muscle strength of 25 per cent in three weeks. Given that steroids can manage, at best, a 10 per cent increase over 10 weeks, some doctors fear there will be considerable implications for the World Anti-Doping Agency (WADA).

'In terms of performance enhancement and sport, it's the holy grail,' Professor Goldspink said.

He claims to have avoided the side-effects that have so far dogged gene therapy. In the past, genetic material designed to boost production of one type of cell has ended up boosting cancerous growths.

This is why tests on humans have been slow in coming and why many have scoffed at the possibility of gene therapy affecting sport. Not any more though. Goldsmith says he is about to sign a multi-million-dollar deal with pharmaceutical giant Novartis to start testing the technique on humans.

Professor Lee Sweeney of the University of Pennsylvania is working on a similar project to help sufferers of muscular dystrophy. His group uses gene therapy to stimulate a different growth hormone called IGF-1 and he confirmed that a human trial is likely to begin in the United States within the year. 'Once you start testing on humans, you'll get rogue doctors in certain countries offering this thing for profit,' he said. 'There's simply too much money to be made.'

Even more troubling for WADA is that, unlike steroids, injecting genes to stimulate MGF or IGF-1 may be undetectable. IGF-1 produced by injecting genetic material is indistinguishable from IGF-1 the body produces naturally through resistance training. The introduced genetic material is detectable but because it is confined to the muscle, testing would involve extracting an actual lump of muscle from every competitor. So, short of taking a pound of flesh, WADA must look elsewhere.

'WADA approached me about developing a test but I'm deeply sceptical,'' said Professor Sweeney. 'You can only test for something if it's in the blood and my job is to make sure it doesn't get into the blood as this will carry it to areas it's not wanted. If we do our jobs properly, it'll be impossible to detect.'

What that means is that WADA are limited to looking for indirect effects. One of their latest research projects is a test for 'protein fingerprints' or abnormal patterns of protein that could only be caused by injected genetic material.

'We're looking for something out of the ordinary, like cells suddenly processing growth hormone when they shouldn't,' said chief scientist Phil Teale. 'I'd envisage that within three years we could detect relevant patterns. But how quickly that translates into an actual testing methodology is hard to say.'

'It's impossible to say whether we will have a fully working test in time for the 2008 Olympics,' said Frederic Donve, WADA's media relations manager. 'We have commissioned five research projects but we can't say when they will produce results.'

A spokesman for UK Sport agreed that although they've 'identified gene doping as a priority' they have no idea when such a test is likely to be operational.

Some believe this is not a battle worth fighting. Andy Miah, author of *Genetically Modified Athletes*, argues that testing for genes would not only be futile but unethical.

'The impetus to find new methods of enhancement is not going to stop,' said Miah. 'We need to draw a line under drug use and consider gene modification as a separate technology. It is a legitimate use of a technology that can improve humanity, not make it less human.'

Whether we try to test for gene doping or not, one subject on which all parties agree is that if athletes aren't using these techniques already they will be soon.

22 May 2005

■ The percentage of adults participating regularly in lifestyle sports increased from 2.5% to 5% between 2001 and 2003. Some 12% of adults want to try lifestyle sports – equivalent to around 5.8 million people. (page 1)

■ Physical activity has been shown to have wide-ranging benefits for all children and young people during their school years including improved concentration, commitment and raised self-esteem. (page 2)

■ Only one in four children is competing against other teams within their school in sports such as hockey and netball. (page 4)

■ A report shows that when England supporters are treated from the outset as fans rather than 'hooligans', they see themselves as on the same side as the police, sharing the same interest in preventing violence. (page 8)

■ More than 85 per cent of sports followers believe that wealthy business people, promoters and celebrities have an increasing influence on sport at the expense of the traditional fan. (page 9)

■ When surveyed, 50% of sports followers said they had never witnessed instances of racist behaviour such as chanting, personal abuse or discrimination in the selection of players or club membership. Only 4% said they had witnessed this kind of incident frequently. (page 10)

■ Last year £786 million in wages alone was paid to 2,347 professional footballers, that's roughly equivalent to the GDP of Mongolia in 2005. (page 11)

■ Ethnic minorities are severely under-represented in the boardrooms and governance arrangements of football clubs and national football organisations. Only one FA Premier League club reported having a non-white board director. (page 12)

■ 85% of participants in an online poll for Football Unites, Racism Divides believed racist chanters should be ejected from football matches. (page 14)

■ The combination of cultural norms, discriminatory practice and women's position in society result in girls and women participating less in sport – although not usually by choice. There is no evidence that women and girls do not like sport. (page 19)

■ Girls aged 7-11 are less than half as likely to take part in physical education and sport compared to boys. (page 20)

■ By the age of 18, 40% of girls have dropped out of sport and physical recreation. (page 20)

■ Television coverage of women's sport makes up only between 0.5% and 6% of all sports coverage. (page 21)

■ Factors such as an athlete's desire to win, the desire to please their coach and family, the glory of victory and the social and economic reward of sporting success often send the athlete in search of a competitive edge. Sometimes this search leads to the use of drugs. (page 29)

■ For athletes, testing is the most effective way of demonstrating that you compete without the use of prohibited substances or methods. (page 31)

■ Under the World Anti-Doping Code, ignorance is no excuse in cases of inadvertent doping – you are solely responsible for checking the status of all medication and substances you use. Athletes that have unwittingly taken a prohibited substance will still face sanctions. (page 31)

■ There is a clear and definitive set of sanctions if you are caught using banned substances. First offenders could face a two-year ban from competing in any sport which has signed the WADA code. Athletes caught a second time may be banned for life. (page 32)

■ More than 6,500 drug tests were undertaken in the UK over the past year (April 2004-March 2005). The final total of 6,520 marks an 11% increase on the previous year (5,876 tests). (page 33)

■ Steroids stimulate the development of male sexual characteristics and the build-up of muscle tissue. They are sometimes used medically to help recovery from an operation and to treat breast cancer. (page 36)

■ Hormones are chemicals that send signals to parts of the body and control certain functions. Hormones are made of peptides which are chains of amino acids. Analogues are man-made chemicals that have the same effect as a hormone. (page 37)

■ Beta-blockers reduce energy and increase fatigue and so would not improve an athlete's performance in sports requiring stamina or strength. However, they have been used by athletes competing in sports requiring control. (page 37)

■ Blood doping increases the amount of red blood cells in the athlete's body, increasing their oxygen-carrying capacity. This can help to improve performance in endurance sports such as cycling and running. (page 38)

GLOSSARY

Anabolic steroids
Natural or man-made substances that act like the hormone testosterone.

Banning order
An order preventing a football fan who is consistently violent from attending matches.

Beta-blockers
A group of drugs used to reduce blood pressure.

Blood doping
A prohibited technique which involves removing some of an athlete's blood a few months before a competition and storing it. The athlete's blood levels return to normal over time and then about a week before the competition the blood is injected back into the athlete.

Commercialisation
The trend in some sports for those involved to be overly concerned with money-making and maximising profits; often, some feel, at the expense of the sport's traditional fans.

Commonwealth Games
Amateur sporting competition held every four years between Commonwealth of Nations member countries (including the UK).

Discrimination
The unjust treatment of a person based on membership of a certain group (e.g. gay, female, Asian etc).

Diuretics
These drugs stimulate the flow of urine, and remove fluids from the body.

Doping
The use of drugs by a sportsman or woman in order to enhance their performance in competition.

Equality
The Equal Opportunities Commission defines equality as 'having a society where everyone is free from assumptions and discrimination based on factors such as gender, race or disability'.

Equity
Equity is about fairness and justice for all those who want to participate in sport. However, unlike equality, equity may also use positive action initiatives and measures to address exisiting inequalities.

Gene doping
This involves transferring genes directly into human cells to blend into an athlete's DNA, in order to enhance muscle growth and increase strength or endurance.

Hooliganism
A term often used to describe violence and unruly behaviour by football supporters.

Inadvertent doping
This occurs when an athlete takes a medication to treat an illness or injury, unaware that it contains a banned substance.

Inclusion
To include in a sport individuals who may be from a group traditionally under-represented in that sport – for example, women, minority ethnic, gay or disabled people.

Narcotic analgesics
Strong painkillers made from opiates taken from the poppy plant.

Olympic Games
A massive sporting competition with a variety of different events, held every four years in a different location. Winning a medal in the Olympics carries great prestige for athletes who compete.

Stimulants
A class of drugs that act on the central nervous system in the same way as the hormone adrenalin, by speeding up parts of the brain and the body's reactions.

Strict liability
The principle of strict liability means an athlete is always held responsible if a banned substance is found in their body, no matter how it got there.

Therapeutic Use Exemption (TUE)
A form giving permission for an athlete to use a banned substance if there is a valid medical reason to do so.

World Anti-Doping Agency (WADA)
An international organisation formed in 1999. Its mission is to promote and coordinate, internationally, the fight against doping in sport.

World Anti-Doping Code
An international set of rules and guidelines devised to protect sport from doping.

UK Sport
UK Sport is the UK's National Anti-Doping Organisation (NADO). These are domestic organisations responsible for planning, collection and management of anti-doping controls in their country.

INDEX

ADDITIONAL RESOURCES

Other Issues titles

If you are interested in researching further the issues raised in *Focus on Sport*, you may want to read the following titles in the **Issues** series as they contain additional relevant articles:

- Vol. 91 *Disability Issues* (ISBN 1 86168 292 1)
- Vol. 101 *Sexuality and Discrimination* (ISBN 1 86168 315 4)
- Vol. 112 *Women, Men and Equality* (ISBN 1 86168 345 6)
- Vol. 113 *Fitness and Health* (ISBN 1 86168 346 4)
- Vol. 114 *Drug Abuse* (ISBN 1 86168 347 2)
- Vol. 115 *Racial Discrimination* (ISBN 1 86168 348 0)

For more information about these titles, visit our website at www.independence.co.uk/publicationslist

Useful organisations

You may find the websites of the following organisations useful for further research:

- 100%Me from UK Sport: www.100percentme.co.uk
- The Austrlian Sports Anti-Doping Authority: www.asada.gov.au
- Child Protection in Sport Unit: www.thecpsu.org.uk
- The Department for Culture, Media and Sport: www.culture.gov.uk
- Sport England: www.sportengland.org
- Sport Scotland: www.sportscotland.org.uk
- Women's Sports Foundation: www.wsf.org.uk

ACKNOWLEDGEMENTS

The publisher is grateful for permission to reproduce the following material.

While every care has been taken to trace and acknowledge copyright, the publisher tenders its apology for any accidental infringement or where copyright has proved untraceable. The publisher would be pleased to come to a suitable arrangement in any such case with the rightful owner.

Chapter One: Sporting Trends
Popularity of lifestyle sports growing fast, © Sport England, *Youngsters play the game – and avoid trouble*, © Telegraph Group Ltd 2006, *School sports*, © NSPCC, *Only a quarter of pupils take part in a team sport*, © 2006 Associated Newspapers Ltd, *More sports playing fields created than ever before*, © Crown copyright is reproduced with the permission of Her Majesty's Stationery Office, *Lost – 34,000 playing fields*, © National Playing Fields Association, *Whatever happened to football hooliganism?*, © Guardian Newspapers Ltd 2005, *Football-related violence seasons 2003/04*, © Crown copyright is reproduced with the permission of Her Majesty's Stationery Office, *'Low-impact' policing key to overcoming hooliganism*, © Economic and Social Research Council, *Commercialisation in sport*, © Telegraph Group Ltd 2006, *Sport – YouGov poll results*, © YouGov, *Footballers' pay*, © Smile.

Chapter Two: Sport and Inclusion
Celebrating diversity and inclusion, © Sport Scotland, *Goal: racial equality in football*, © Commission for Racial Equality, *Racism alive and kicking in England, say UEFA*, © Guardian Newspapers Ltd 2006, *Asians can play football*, © National Asians in Football Forum, *Football to boot out homophobic fans*, © Guardian Newspapers Ltd 2005, *The place of gender equity in sport*, © Women's Sports Foundation, *Facts, trends and statistics*, © Women's Sports Foundation, *Women, sport and the media*, © Women's Sports Foundation, *A level playing field*, © The Football Association.

Chapter Three: Drug Abuse in Sport
History of drugs in sport, © Australian Government, *Anti-doping timeline*, © Australian Government, *Drug-free sport*, © Crown copyright is reproduced with the permission of Her Majesty's Stationery Office, *Why athletes take drugs*, © Australian Government, *Testing time as anti-doping laws get tougher*, © Telegraph Group Ltd 2006, *The World Anti-Doping Code*, © UK Sport, *Athlete's advice*, © UK Sport, *Drug tests in sport up 11% last year*, © UK Sport, *Demand for doping ban to be doubled*, © Telegraph Group Ltd 2006, *Gym drugs*, © TheSite.org, *Drugs and methods in sport – effects and risks*, © UK Sport, *Gene therapy promises the holy grail*, © Telegraph Group Ltd 2006.

Photographs and illustrations:
Pages 1, 17, 30, 39: Simon Kneebone; pages 4, 25, 38: Don Hatcher; pages 9, 27, 29: Angelo Madrid; pages 12, 23: Bev Aisbett; page 13: Pumpkin House.

Craig Donnellan
Cambridge
April, 2006